Henry Augustus Boardman

The Higher Life

Doctrine of Sanctification

Henry Augustus Boardman

The Higher Life
Doctrine of Sanctification

ISBN/EAN: 9783744774710

Printed in Europe, USA, Canada, Australia, Japan

Cover: Foto ©Lupo / pixelio.de

More available books at **www.hansebooks.com**

THE "HIGHER LIFE" DOCTRINE

OF

SANCTIFICATION,

TRIED BY THE

WORD OF GOD.

BY

HENRY A. BOARDMAN, D.D.,

AUTHOR OF "THE APOSTOLICAL SUCCESSION," "THE BIBLE IN THE COUNTING-HOUSE," "THE BIBLE IN THE FAMILY," "THE GREAT QUESTION," ETC.

PHILADELPHIA:
PRESBYTERIAN BOARD OF PUBLICATION,
1334 CHESTNUT STREET.

Entered according to Act of Congress, in the year 1877, by
THE TRUSTEES OF THE
PRESBYTERIAN BOARD OF PUBLICATION,
In the Office of the Librarian of Congress, at Washington.

WESTCOTT & THOMSON,
Stereotypers and Electrotypers, Philada.

THE "HIGHER LIFE" DOCTRINE

OF

SANCTIFICATION

PREFACE.

"*The Higher Christian Life,*" by the Rev. William E. Boardman, was published some twenty years ago. It has been followed by numerous books and tracts of a kindred type. An efficient *Propaganda,* established in the interest of the new creed, has given it wide currency through the medium of Lectures, Addresses, and "Holiness Meetings." Its Apostles of both sexes, sincere and earnest in their faith and exemplary in life, labor with unflagging zeal to win converts to the cause,—and with such alleged success, that they now report "many thousands in many lands" as having embraced it. This result is not surprising. Where "Perfection" is the glittering prize, and darling *Self* is not only suitor, but judge, jury, counsel, and sole witness, it is easy to forecast the verdict. But all the more needful is it that the case should be removed to some other forum, and tried before a less partial tribunal. Up to this period, the "Higher Life" teachers have had the public ear very much to themselves. Occasional protests have been put forth, and the religious Journals have discussed with marked ability certain aspects of the scheme. But, in so far as is known to the present writer, not a single volume devoted to a careful dissection of the system has been issued either in England, where they claim numerous adherents, or in our own country. As the natural consequence, there is much curiosity and *bewilderment* abroad as to the real character of these speculations, and how far they may have a Scriptural basis. Pastors are frequently met with questions about the "Higher Life," on the part of parishioners whose consciences have been disturbed by the lectures or books of its advocates: and there are, unfortunately, no publications to which these inquirers can be referred for a solution of their difficulties.

The time, then, seems to have come when *some* one should take up the doctrine of "Perfect Sanctification," and compare it with the word of

God—the more so, as the latest expositions of the system with which we have been favored disclose that insidious tendency toward a widening departure from "the faith once delivered to the saints," which is the inborn bias of all serious error. It was from no seeking of my own that this service was devolved upon me. So far from it, I have conscientiously sought to escape from it, in the face of manifold appeals urgently pressed, for the past three years: for it seemed a very ungracious office, to become the censor of a company of devout people who are honestly striving to bring their fellow-Christians up to a higher standard of piety. But Providence at length interposed in a manner which seemed to annul all personal considerations, and to shut me up to the performance of a very unwelcome duty. No alternative was left me, but to attempt to bring the theology of this active and growing school, to the test of "the law and the testimony."

Of the manner in which the examination has been conducted, it is for others to judge. Two features of this inquiry require a word of notice. One is, the fulness of the quotations from the

Higher Life books. They are made thus ample for two reasons: First, that uninitiated readers may learn what the system is—a problem which, to the author's personal knowledge, has baffled very intelligent and experienced Christians. And secondly, that the authors in question may have no occasion to complain that their views have been misrepresented. The other feature, is, the frequent recurrence of the same trains of thought, not to say of the same phraseology. The explanation of this will be found in the very peculiar structure of the theory under review. That theory has its centre and circumference in a solitary act of faith. This act of faith comes into view in all relations. It is interlaced with every topic, and made the pivot upon which the whole mechanism turns. It was unavoidable, therefore, that it should be met on its constant reappearance, and its fallacy in every aspect exposed. This was due no less to those who may incautiously have accepted the system, than to others who have not yet been allured from the "old paths."

As an offset to the large citations from these authors, liberal extracts have been introduced from the works of Divines whose names are known and honored throughout Protestant Christendom. The motive for this has been two-fold. First, that it may be distinctly seen that the views of sanctification maintained in this volume represent the common faith of evangelical believers; and, secondly, that the views thus set forth may, with the greater urgency, claim the serious attention of persons who have embraced the Higher Life delusion. To those who have watched the progress of this movement, it is quite apparent that many have fallen in with it who have not carefully inquired into its alleged correspondence with the word of God; some, in fact, after getting further light, have frankly acknowledged that this was the misstep which had led them astray. It seems reasonable to believe, that among this large class of disciples, there must be many who will feel like re-examining their new faith, on learning that it has been pronounced unscriptural and dangerous by a large number of the most eminent and godly teachers known to the Church since the Apostolic age. This hope may be indulged even in presence of the historical fact, that it has always been the tendency of Perfectionism, in whatever form, to inspire a self-confidence which is well-nigh invincible to argument. But truth, after all, is mightier than error. The promise is, "When He, the Spirit of truth, is come, He will guide you into all (the) truth." And we have no right to distrust either His power or His willingness to recover *any* who may inadvertently have erred in respect to this or any other doctrine of His holy word.

It may be worth while to say, that no wholesale condemnation of the "Higher Life" literature is intended. There is a generous leaven of faithful exhortation and Scriptural counsel diffused through the mass, which has no doubt been helpful to many readers. And there are able and attractive writers, more or less identified in the public mind with this scheme, whose sterling essays in behalf of a more simple and implicit faith, and an entire consecration to God, betray no affinity whatever with its obnoxious peculiarities. This latter class will not be found proclaiming as *new*, a style of teaching on the duty of coming to Christ without delay, "taking Christ as our all in all," and other kindred topics, which is preached, and prayed, and sung, in ten thousand churches every Sunday. Their aim is one with that of the school in question, but they are employing quite other methods and in a different spirit, to win their fellow-Christians to the culture and practice of "a closer walk with God."

The subject of Christian Sanctification—the growing assimilation of the soul to the Divine image through the indwelling of the Holy Ghost—is eminently one to be approached with a reverent and chastened spirit. In this spirit I have at least aimed to consider it in the following pages. It is my humble prayer, that if the sentiments here inculcated be not derived from the unerring word, they may fall to the ground "as water that cannot be gathered up again;" and that if the teaching of the book reflect, in any fitting measure, the mind of the Spirit, He may be pleased to use it as a means of good. H. A. B.

1311 SPRUCE STREET, PHILADELPHIA,
   May, 1877.

CONTENTS.

                                                              PAGE

PREFACE... 9

CHAPTER I.

LOFTY CLAIMS.. 19

    Sanctification by faith "a newly-discovered doctrine"—Eighteen centuries of twilight—Luther misinterpreted.

CHAPTER II.

THE OLD DOCTRINE AND THE NEW...................... 29

    Sanctification according to the Scriptures—According to the Higher Life Scheme.

CHAPTER III.

FAITH MISAPPREHENDED IN ITS NATURE AND OBJECTS.. 38

    Faith "not a grace"—Wrong to pray for it—Plenary ability—No recognition of the Holy Spirit—Marshall on Sanctification—Jenks's Prayer—A faith unknown to inspired teachers.

CHAPTER IV.

THE WILL NOT OMNIPOTENT—"CONSECRATION"...... 59

Consecration everything—Faith mistaking its object—Faith without feeling—"The will, king"—The usurper dethroned.

CHAPTER V.

FURTHER MISTAKES AS TO FAITH AND CONSECRATION...... 73

Unwarrantable assumptions—Full assurance, scriptural and unscriptural.

CHAPTER VI.

NOVELTIES IN SCRIPTURE INTERPRETATION—MYSTICISM...... 81

Mystical teachings—Ominous omissions—1 Cor. 1 : 30; Col. 3 : 3; Gal. 2 : 20.

CHAPTER VII.

MORE TEXTS MISINTERPRETED—ROMANS VII...... 98

1 John 1 : 7—Paul in Romans seventh, a poor Christian—"Dead to sin"—Chalmers on Romans sixth and seventh—Bishop Hopkins—Romans seventh paraphrased.

CHAPTER VIII.

"Half-Truths" — Commands and Promises — Prayer.. 124

The Christian life a cheerful service—Misrepresented—Texts bi-sected—Errors respecting prayer.

CHAPTER IX.

Passivity vs. Activity—Faith Restricted, and Scripture Slighted... 137

The in-dwelling of Christ—Sanctification through the truth—Chalmers on Phil. 2 : 12, 13—Making Christ "responsible"—All Scripture profitable for growth in grace.

CHAPTER X.

The Lessons of 1 John, Chapter I...................... 159

Dangerous wresting of Scripture—Self-deception—Scott—Daillé—Marshall.

CHAPTER XI.

The Law Debased—Sin, no Sin—The Lord's Prayer... 176

Dr. Alden—A flexible law no law—"Consciousness" an untrustworthy guide—Newton and the slave-trade—God's law applied—Beyond the Lord's Prayer.

CHAPTER XII.

THE SCHEME INCOMPATIBLE WITH THE GENERAL TONE OF THE INSPIRED WORD—PILGRIM'S PROGRESS.. 196

 Higher Life consecration and sinlessness unknown to the New Testament—If true, Pilgrim's Progress literally a "dream."

CHAPTER XIII.

A BLEAK SYSTEM FOR DOUBTING AND DESPONDING BELIEVERS.. 204

 Rough Surgery—Casuistical Theology—Diversities of Gifts—Humility, true and false.

CHAPTER XIV.

THE SCHEME DEFICIENT IN SOLID COMFORT FOR GOD'S CHILDREN—SELF-DECEPTION—EGOISM.......... 224

 Specious vs. Scriptural teaching—Leighton—Many Doubters—The only true resource.

CHAPTER XV.

HIGHER LIFE EXAMPLES.. 244

 Not drawn from "Christian Biography"—Not tested by time—Perfect Happiness here not proposed to us—

William Archer Butler—"What do ye more than others?"

CHAPTER XVI.

                                                             PAGE
Trustworthy Experiences—Conclusion............ 260
    Owen—Bunyan—John Newton—Alexander—McCheyne—Wilberforce—Gurney—Adelaide Newton—Simeon—"The old, old story."

THE "HIGHER LIFE" DOCTRINE

OF

SANCTIFICATION.

CHAPTER I.

LOFTY CLAIMS.

It is a hopeful sign that in this restless, money-making age, CHRISTIAN SANCTIFICATION should have become a subject of wide-spread inquiry and discussion. No subject can be named which is of more universal and urgent importance; and if certain of the views so assiduously pressed of late upon the public attention derived their inspiration from the word of God, the prominence assigned to them might be just cause for congratulation among Christians of every name. Whether they really bear the King's sign-manual has become a question of such gravity as not merely to invite, but to demand, the most careful consideration on the part of all who would guard the precious truths deposited in the ark of the covenant from misapprehension or perversion.

This is due to the sponsors of what is known as the theory of the "HIGHER CHRISTIAN LIFE." They bear the credentials of God's own children. Their genuine culture, their earnest piety, their intense devotion to the grand mission they suppose to have been confided to them, of lifting up the Church to a higher plane in the spiritual realm, entitle them personally to the respect and confidence which have been so freely accorded to them. When such persons speak, they have a right to be heard. That they have spoken, that their many-voiced utterances are perpetually going forth from the pulpit, the rostrum and the press, is known and read of all men. Of the quality of these utterances it must be said that they are as authoritative in their tone as they are lofty in their assumptions. No one familiar with them can be surprised that even instructed believers should in some cases have been captivated by them, and that Christian pastors should be daily asked by serious-minded parishioners, "What new doctrine is this? Certain strange things are brought to our ears, and we would know whether they be of the faith once delivered to the saints, or mere human inventions." How could it be otherwise? The pretensions of these teachers to superior illumination would seem incredible, were they not put forth with an endless iteration and in terms which admit of no misconception. Listen to these extraordinary averments concerning the renewing and sanctification of sinners:

"It is only one hundred years since the great truth of the new birth as a distinct experience, the privilege of all, began to receive its full power of application to the heart and life of the Church. . . . To the great central doctrine of justification by faith, revived before in the Reformation, the fact of the new birth as an experience for all was now (one hundred years ago) added to the faith of the Church in the great awakening." Again, referring to the experimental "apprehension of the principle of sanctification by faith as the privilege of all," "Why has the fact not had greater prominence in the past? Why have eighteen centuries been allowed to roll away before it is brought distinctly and prominently before the mind of the Church? The answer is, that until now the time has never come for it. Now is the time. . . . And yet until now the time has never come to give it fully the prominence which now it is destined to take and to hold in the future history and progress of the kingdom of God in the world."*

Well may the *Princeton Review* (Oct., 1860), after quoting these passages, remark: "How any one, with a whole heaven of light streaming upon him in brightness above that of the noon-day sun, with every Protestant Confession, every doctrinal symbol of the evangelical Church from the Reformation down to this hour, proclaiming its clear and emphatic denial, could ever have put on record a statement like this [concerning the new birth], it surpasses our ability to conceive." "What system of Protestant Biblical theology has ever been written, what Protestant evangelical Church has ever adopted a Confession, in which this very idea of sanctification by faith in Christ is not adopted as one of its fundamental truths? . . . A man might as well lift up his head and inquire, Why have eighteen centuries been allowed to roll away before the sun-light is brought prominently before the public eye?"

Some light has been shed within the last fif-

---

* *The Higher Christian Life*, by the Rev. W. E. Boardman. Boston, 1859.

teen years upon the meaning they attach to the phrase "sanctification by faith," or, as otherwise expressed, "Holiness through faith." There is still a vital element in the theory which needs elucidation, and there is very much which, as ample observation has shown, makes the whole scheme misty and perplexing to the common mind. But nothing has been published in abatement of the startling asseveration, that they have been initiated into "a mystery which has been hid from ages and from generations;" that the high function has been entrusted to them of revealing to the Christian world the way out of bondage into liberty; out of perpetual conflict to lasting victory; out of habitual anxiety and unsated longings to unbroken serenity and rest; out of dark, or at best glimmering, twilight into the bracing air of a cloudless heaven. These contrasts define in no exaggerated terms the comparison they draw between their own happy lot and the condition of the great mass even of those whom they recognize as sincere believers. Had they contented themselves with saying that the evangelical Church, with its profusion of active labors, is still sadly deficient in spirituality, and that multitudes of disciples fail to live up to the ful measure of their privilege, the statements would have provoked no controversy; but when they represent "ordinary Christians" generally as continuing in a state of degrading servitude; as not taking Christ for their all in all; as knowing little or nothing experimentally of the joy of pardon and acceptance with God; as rarely seeking, and yet more rarely attaining, a full assurance of faith; and, by reason hereof, bringing dishonor upon the glorious gospel of the grace of God;—we find nothing to justify or excuse such allegations either in the self-confidence of those who utter them, or in the pity they bestow upon their less-favored brethren. Still less are we disposed to listen without protest when told, as we are, that outside of their own limited circle, the people of God have not learned, what is certainly one of the earliest and simplest lessons in experimental religion—that it is their duty and privilege "to take Christ as their sanctification."

Having been somewhat familiar with the controversies, theological and ecclesiastical, of the last forty years, the writer can recall no sect or school which has come before the sisterhood of churches with higher pretensions than these. Stripped of superfluous verbiage, we are gravely asked to believe that the Christian Church has for eighteen centuries been left in the dark as to the great central doctrine of Sanctification; that the learned and pious divines at whose feet, next to those of Christ and his apostles, disciples have been most willing to sit; intrepid Missionaries who have carried the banner of the cross into the benighted regions of paganism; and thousands of martyrs who have sealed their testimony with their blood, have died without any full apprehension of the true way of Sanctification. What then becomes of the promised mission, indwelling, and guidance of the Holy Spirit? Do not these writers see what indignity they are doing alike to the Saviour as the Head of the Church, and to the blessed Comforter? If God has for ages left His people in ignorance of the only method in which they can be effectually freed from the dominion of sin, what assurance can there be that they have not mistaken the method of pardon also? If misled as to Sanctification, why not as to Justification? If the Reformed Churches have all misapprehended the meaning of Scripture as to the vital matter of personal holiness, who can deny that their Creeds and Confessions may be equally at fault on many other fundamental points?

Unless the writer has failed, after the patient study of a large series of their publications, to understand our new teachers, these remarks do them no injustice. They do not claim that their theory of perfect sanctification is in harmony with the current traditions of the Historic Churches. They claim the very reverse. They produce it as a novelty—a novelty, however, simply because Churches and individuals have somehow failed to see it, albeit written in letters of light upon every page of the New Testament. As if in practical acknowledgment of its incongruity with the ordinary experience of believers, they pass by the rich stores of Christian Biography, from Chrysostom and Augustine to Martyn, Brainerd and Payson, and derive their illustrations chiefly from recent and nameless examples, and pre-eminently from their own personal exercises. It is true that in one of the opening chapters of the book just quoted, a formal attempt is made to show that Martin Luther's experience was in the line of their speculations. Referring to the well-known incident, that as the great Reformer was climbing up the Santa Scala at Rome, the prophet's utterance, "The just shall live by faith," fell upon his ears as in tones of thunder, and sent him flying in haste from that scene of superstitious devotion, the author claims, that what he discovered at that pregnant moment, was, that the believer "lives, *i. e.* is *kept alive, by faith.*" He had already accepted Christ as his justification. Now it is revealed to him that he must take Christ as his sanctification also. And *this* revelation it was which so agitated and overwhelmed him, and which transformed him from that hour into quite another man. It is apparent that the writer penned his account of this transaction, with Merle d'Aubigné's *History of the Reformation* open before him, wherein it is expressly stated, that what wrought so mightily in the heart of Luther, was a sudden and distinct apprehension of the righteousness of Christ as the sole and complete ground of a sinner's *justification*. Certainly he obtained at the same time, for God has joined these two things together, a clearer view of the union of the soul with Christ as the source of all spiritual life and strength and comfort. But it is passing strange how any writer, and especially one who claims to be leading the "higher Christian life," can represent this, in contradistinction from the revelation of Christ's justifying righteousness, as the grand, central truth disclosed to the astonished mind of the Reformer. No ingenuity can warp the experience either of Luther or D'Aubigné (see the same book) into accord with the notions of a complete sanctification as inculcated by this new school of Perfectionists: and it were better not to put such witnesses on the stand, if they are not to be allowed to testify "the truth, the *whole* truth, and nothing but the truth."

In styling the scheme a "novelty," it is not meant that Perfectionism is an error of recent birth. Not only has it often appeared and re-appeared within the enclosure of orthodox Churches, but it has been the cardinal doctrine of various sects which have sprung up like Jonah's gourd, and like it have presently withered. That it should find permanent entertainment with a great and honored evangelical Communion, is a phenomenon which need not here be discussed. But the Perfectionism with which we have to do as an aggressive and proselyting system, is of another type—so unique in fact, in one essential feature, as to warrant its claim to the high distinction of being a new revelation. Peradventure it may turn out, that wherein the scheme is new, it is not Scriptural; and wherein it is Scriptural, it is not new.

CHAPTER II.

THE OLD DOCTRINE AND THE NEW.

According to the word of God, men are by nature, "children of wrath," "dead in trespasses and sins." The two great evils under which we labor, are, subjection to the penalty of the Divine law, and corruption of heart. From the one we are delivered by the work of Christ for us: from the other, by the work of the Holy Spirit in us. The new birth is an instantaneous change wrought in the soul by the direct agency of the Holy Ghost. It is described as a resurrection, as a new creation, and by other terms which show that it is a transition from death to life, the mightiest transformation of which the human soul is susceptible. Notwithstanding the prominence given to it in both the Old and the New Testaments, the Higher Life literature, while recognizing, rarely dwells upon it. Justification is an act of God, imputing to the sinner, who receives the same by faith, the righteousness of Christ, as his sole ground of pardon and acceptance. It is a forensic act, completed at once, and radically changing the sinner's *state*. Regeneration is an inward act, complete at once, and radically changing his *character*. Sanctification is the work of God's free grace, carrying forward the blessed amelioration, which is commenced in regeneration; and by it we are renewed in the whole man, and are enabled more and more to die unto sin and to live unto righteousness. Unlike justification, it is a work, not an act; progressive; and more thorough in some persons than in others. It is variously attributed to God absolutely, and to the Second Person of the Trinity, but usually to the Third, who is constantly affirmed to be the Author of all holy exercises. As the great Executive of the new Dispensation, the Holy Spirit works faith and repentance in the soul at the beginning; leads the sinner to Christ; unites him with Christ; through the study of the Scriptures, prayer, and providences, inspires and nourishes his love, peace, humility, joy, and other graces, and (not without many lets and drawbacks,) gradually assimilates him to the Divine image. Under this tutelage, "such as truly believe in the Lord Jesus, and love Him in sincerity, endeavoring to walk in all good conscience before Him, may in this life be certainly assured that they are in a state of grace, and may rejoice in the hope of the glory of God." "This infallible assurance doth not so belong to the essence of faith, but that a true believer may wait long, and conflict with many difficulties before he be partaker of it: yet being enabled by the Spirit to know the things that are freely given him of God, he may, without extraordinary revelation, in the right use of ordinary means, attain thereunto."* To this blessed estate, very many believers do attain, and *that*, not unfrequently, soon after their engrafting into Christ: and from thousands of pulpits and in countless publications, all are instructed that it is their duty and privilege to aspire after it.

It is proper to add, in offering this concise statement of the accepted theology, that, diverse as are the factors in regeneration and justification, these two essential transactions are never disjoined. It is not possible that a justified sinner should be left, even for a moment, in a condition of spiritual death; nor a renewed sinner under the condemnation of the law. By one and the same act of faith, the soul takes Christ as its righteousness and its sanctification; as the ground of its hope, and the source of its new life; as the Author not only, but the Finisher, of its faith; as the spring of

* *Westminster Confession*, ch. viii.

its vitality and growth, as really as the vine alone sustains its branches, or the head the members.

The summary thus given is unfortunately rendered necessary by the gross injustice which is habitually done by Higher Life writers, to the views and experiences of "ordinary Christians." If this proceeds from ignorance, as charity bids us believe, there is no breach of charity in saying, that it is an ignorance which is neither innocent nor harmless. What *they* really teach is this:— Believers in general have received Jesus Christ simply as their justification. "They have learned *only* that their sins are forgiven through faith in the atonement of Jesus. They have not yet learned that Jesus, through faith in His name is the Deliverer from the power of sin, as well as from its penalty. They sigh and groan in their bondage as if there was no deliverance this side the grave. Not knowing that Jesus can deliver them, they turn with a sigh toward death as their deliverer from the power of this death, as if death was the sanctifier or the sanctification of the children of God."*

"The grand difference between the two classes is, that the one has and the other has not found Jesus as a present Saviour from the present power

* W. E. Boardman.

of sin." "Once we were in the seventh chapter of Romans; but thanks be to God through our Lord Jesus Christ, who has given us deliverance from the body of death, we have now found our way out of the bondage of the seventh, into the sweet liberty of the eighth." "The dead body (of sin) is dropped." "Bondage is gone, freedom is come. Sighs give place to joys, fears to hopes."* The seventh chapter of Romans is a grievous offence to this school: they miss no occasion of making a thrust at it,—as we shall see.

The deliverance thus commemorated, is a deliverance from all conscious sin. They do not assert, with the Oberlin Perfectionists, that absolute holiness—holiness which meets the full requirements of the decalogue—is ever attained in this life. They would hardly venture to say with that courageous sect, "We have evidence just as conclusive, that perfect and perpetual holiness is promised to Christians, as we have that it is required of them. We have the same evidence from Scripture that all Christians may, and that some of them will, attain to a state of entire sanctification in this life, that they will attain to that state in heaven." This is the only consistent ground, the only logical deduction from the principle, that

* W. E. Boardman.

the commands and promises of God's word are the proper measurement of the personal holiness assured to believers in this world. Shrinking from this assumption, they challenge for themselves an exemption from all known sin, even sins of the heart. It would fill several pages to recite the passages in which they affirm that they are now "cleansed from *all* (conscious) sin;" that they are "dead to sin;" that they are "living fully up to the light God has given them;" that there are no longer any "cross-currents" in their breasts; that the "body of sin" in them "is destroyed;" that they are "filled with the Spirit;" that with the shield of faith which they carry, they not only can, but do, "quench *all* the fiery darts of the Wicked;" and that they are "lost and swallowed up in Christ."* These protestations, which fall upon the common ear with so startling a sound, are qualified in two ways. (1) This spiritual perfection is referable entirely to the indwelling Christ. Having taken Him as their sanctification, they have devolved all their duties, trials, and conflicts upon Him. "I have done working. I simply resign my will to His will. And He does it all." (2) This lofty estate is theirs only so long as they keep renewing the act

* See the writings of "R. P. S" and "H. W. S.," passim.

of faith through which it becomes theirs. One instance is mentioned of a believer whose "obedience (according to his own report) had been kept at the extreme verge of his light for *twenty-one years.*" Another had lived in his tabernacle on this Mount of Transfiguration (for what other spot of earth could boast such a tabernacle?) for fourteen years. But, as might be expected, there are many "failures." And large discourse is employed to point out how "*the blessing,*" when lost, is to be recovered.

This is the chosen phrase for designating the unsinning state which distinguishes the higher Christian life. "Have you obtained 'the blessing'? Have you got beyond the conflict with indwelling sin? Have you entered into the appointed Rest? Are you made perfect in holiness?" The way to achieve this, is simply to "take Christ as your sanctification, as you have already taken Him for your justification." The unsophisticated reader of the Bible finds "growth in grace" a gradual process like growth in plants and animals—albeit the vital force is derived from Christ. United to Christ by that faith which is itself the "gift of God" (Eph. 2:8), the renewed sinner becomes thereby a member of His mystical body. The Holy Spirit thenceforth dwells in him.

The Spirit has come to replace in the Church the personal presence of the Saviour. His function is, to receive of the things of Christ and show them to His own; to lead them into the truth; and to sanctify them through the truth. The Spirit being, officially, in subordination to Christ, where He is, Christ is. The grace He communicates to the believer, is derived from Christ, the Head. This grace, bestowed according to His good pleasure, keeps alive, invigorates, and matures, the life of God in the soul. That this is done by degrees, is a truth so interwoven with the texture of both Testaments, that to eliminate it would be to change the whole character of the Book.

Not so, however, believe our new guides. By a single act of consecration, Christ becomes your perfect sanctification. So completely does He take possession of your heart, that His life is henceforth your life. Instantaneously every weight falls from your shoulders; all sin vanishes from your breast; the flesh ceases to lust against the Spirit; in so far as your own strivings are concerned, your warfare is accomplished and your victory won; and, to the extent of your consciousness, you are *absolutely holy*. Should your faith fail, you may decline from this beatific state.

And with further light, you may detect something wrong within of which you do not now take cognizance. But in so far as you see yourself, or can search the depths of your innermost nature, you are able to say, " I am pure from my sin."

CHAPTER III.

FAITH MISAPPREHENDED IN ITS NATURE AND OBJECTS.

It is equitable that these teachers should be permitted to speak for themselves. In a tract (by H. W. S.) entitled "*Faith*," * written expressly "to make it so plain that no one need have any difficulty in understanding it," we encounter views of human ability with which Pelagius himself would have been satisfied.

"By very many faith is considered to be a gracious disposition of the soul, wrought by the Holy Ghost in answer to wrestling prayer." "Others look upon faith as though it were a sort of *thing*, received also in answer to wrestling prayer—a sort of spiritual commodity, done up as it were in packages, and labeled, 'Faith,' to be stowed away in the heart, ready to use as a species of coin with which to buy God's gifts, or an equivalent to induce Him to part with them." (To pause for a moment at this sentence,—is this

* " *Willard Tract Repository.*"

representation true? Can the author cite the feeblest testimony, written or oral, which will warrant it? If there be authority for it, let it be produced. If it be meant as a burlesque, it is marvellous that a Christian who has "attained," can trifle on so grave a subject.) To resume— "All, almost without exception, *pray* for faith, entreating God to give them this priceless gift, and wait and watch for the realization of its having been given them. . . . Now one thing is very plain. If God has already given us something, and we persist in ignoring this fact, and go on asking Him yet to give it, we shall certainly get no answer to such prayers as these. God has already given me a hand; if I wanted to pick up anything, it would be useless for me to begin to ask Him afresh to give me a hand; no answer would ever come to such a prayer as that, let it be prayed ever so fervently and sincerely. What I must do is, simply to use, by the force of my will, the hand He has already given me. And it is just so with faith. God has likewise already given me faith. To every human being He has given the power to believe. When the moment comes, then, in which I am called upon to believe something, I must not ask afresh for this power, but must use, by the force of my will, the power

He has already given me. If I am ignorant of the fact that He has given it, and devote myself to earnest prayer in order to obtain it, I cannot wonder that these prayers seem fruitless.

"Our Lord himself has given us a striking lesson on exactly this point, in that memorable passage in Luke 17 : 5, 6, where the disciples offered just such a prayer—'Lord, increase our faith.' His answer, instead of being an assurance that He would do so, was rather a reproof, to the purport, that it was not *more* faith they needed, but only to use what they had; for He said the least grain of faith, as tiny as a grain of mustard-seed, 'the least of all seeds,' could pluck up trees by the root, and overcome the very forces of Nature herself. What, then, could they want with more?

"That the power to believe must have been given before the command to believe came, is a self-evident fact. God's commands are not grievous, but this surely would be, did it come to beings who had no power to obey it. From the fact, therefore, that God has made us responsible for believing, that He is always commanding us to do it, and invariably censures us when we do not, and that He has made unbelief the only condemning sin; from these facts, I say, we are forced to conclude that the power to believe has been given us, and is ours. God has said to us in plain terms to this import, 'Here is one thing you can do, and it is therefore the only thing that I demand from you, but this I do demand—believe, believe, believe!' If, however, the power to believe were not ours, then, instead of being told to believe, we ought to have been told to pray, to ask for faith; and we would surely have been expected to wait until God might be pleased to give it to us. And thus the responsibility would have been shifted off our shoulders on to His. For if a man has no hand, he is surely not to blame if he does not pick up something; and if a man has no faith, he is equally not to blame if he does not believe something. And, practically, those who hold the common view of faith do thus shift the responsibility, and feel at liberty to sit down in helplessness, and wait for the bestowal of this absolutely necessary grace. God says, 'Believe;' they say, 'Pray;' and then they wonder that their way is not more successful.

"Again, therefore, let me repeat it: we have the power to believe, and we are responsible for believing. It is the one thing *we* have got to do. All the rest God has undertaken. This only is our part. And in order to be saved we must do it—we ourselves for ourselves, and not another for us.

"And when I say we have the power to believe, it is the same as saying we have faith, for faith is simply believing things. Faith in man and faith in God are precisely the same thing in their nature; the difference consisting only in the different persons believed in. Faith in man links us on to and makes us one with mere humanity; faith in God links us on to and makes us one with divinity." . . . "Faith, then, is *not a grace*, nor a gracious disposition. . . . Neither are there different kinds of faith. Men talk about a feeling faith, and a living faith, and a saving faith, and an intellectual faith, and an historical faith, and a dead faith; but God talks about believing what He says, and this is the only kind of faith the Bible mentions. The difference is not in the kind of believing, but in the thing or person believed in. . . . It is the object of our faith that makes the mighty difference."

(1) Here we have, in its baldest form, the rationalistic maxim, that ability is the measure of obligation. If God has required us to do what we are unable to do, the responsibility is His, not ours. The statement, it will be seen, is unqualified. It applies equally to the uncon-

verted and the converted. And it would be true if the case were like that of a man "who, having no hand, should be required to pick up something;" or like that of an idiot who should be required to conduct a process of reasoning. But the case is widely different. Man has all the faculties essential to obedience, and the needful opportunities for exercising them. But in his unrenewed state he neither perceives the excellency and glory of the Divine character, nor has any right disposition God-ward. Herein lies his inability, while his conscience attests his responsibility. What is more, both these conditions still attach, in their measure, to the child of God. Notwithstanding his desires are all heavenward, and he longs to be wholly conformed to God, sin is his "grief and thrall;" he is conscious on the one hand, that he *ought* to become on the moment a sinless man, and on the other that he can no more do this than he can create a world. Nor will the apostles of the "Higher Life" bear this test. They claim that they are free from "*conscious* sin." But God's command is, "Be ye holy, for I am holy." Can they elude the obligation of this command? Can they comply with it?

(2) Faith, we are told, is "not a grace;" and

as a grace is a gift, it is no gift; and therefore we "*are not to pray* for it." No one denies that the faith which has for its object a speculative or mathematical proposition, may be simply an intellectual exercise. But when faith has to do with propositions in morals, or with promises and threatenings, it is no longer simple but complex, involving as well the affections and will as the understanding. Especially does this hold in respect to the faith that is connected with salvation. For to believe in Christ is to *trust* in Him; and trust is no mere act of the understanding. Moreover, saving faith differs from an historical or merely speculative faith, not only " in the object or person believed," but in the *evidence* upon which it is founded. A blind man is led to a tower and the scene before him is described by a friend with the utmost accuracy. Presently, by a surgical operation, his sight is restored. How different his apprehensions of the panorama now, from his previous conceptions. So a fine painting, as seen by candlelight, in the twilight, and at noonday, becomes virtually three different paintings. Everything depends upon the light—the evidence. A man, religiously trained, believes all that the Scriptures say concerning the Lord Jesus Christ; but he "sees no beauty in Him that he should desire Him." The Holy Spirit renews his heart and reveals the Saviour to him in His true character; and instantly his heart goes out in trusting love towards Jesus of Nazareth who stands before him as the "chief among ten thousand, the One altogether lovely." The Person is the same. The statements believed are the same. But a new light has fallen upon the scene, and the beholder has been endowed with a susceptibility to spiritual truth and beauty, to which he was before a stranger. The same truth, it has been aptly said, may be believed on different grounds. "One may believe the Christian system simply because others around him believe it, and he has been brought up to receive it without question: this is the faith of credulity. Another may believe it on the ground of its external evidence, *e. g.* of miracle, prophecy, history, its logical consistency as a system, or its plausibility as a theory in accounting for the phenomena of creation and providence: this is speculative faith. Another may believe, because the truths of the Bible recommend themselves to his reason and conscience, and accord with his inward experience: this faith is founded on moral evidence. There is another faith founded on the intrinsic excellence, beauty, and suitableness of the truth, from a sense and love of its moral excellence: this is spiritual faith, which is the '*gift of God.*'"*

It follows that the account of faith contained in the tract quoted above, will not cohere with the teachings of the New Testament. The Saviour and His apostles do, indeed, constantly exhort and command men to "believe." But they are far from telling them that they have plenary ability to believe, and that they can by a single act of consecration free themselves from all sin. So far from it, they teach that saving faith is the "faith of the *operation of God.*" (Col. 2 : 12.) They ascribe it to the direct exertion of the Divine Omnipotence upon the heart. "That ye may know . . . what is the exceeding greatness of His power to us-ward who believe, according to the *working of His mighty power* which He wrought in Christ when He raised Him from the dead, and set Him at His own right hand in the heavenly places." (Eph. 1 : 18–20.) The power which raised up Christ from the grave must be put forth to work faith in the human heart. This is simply saying, in another form, that we must be born of the Spirit; and that it is only as we are enlightened, guided, and strengthened by the Spirit, we can really understand or savingly em-

* *The Way of Life*, by Dr. Charles Hodge.

brace the truth as it is in Jesus. That there is a new principle, a gracious disposition, imparted in regeneration, wherein are the rudiments of *all* holy affections and desires, and that faith is rightly represented as a "grace," has been the common doctrine of believers from the Day of Pentecost until now.

And so, saving faith has been accurately defined, as that spiritual discernment of the excellence and beauty of Divine truth, more especially of the truth relating to the Lord Jesus Christ in His Redeeming work, and that cordial embrace and acceptance of it, which are wrought in the heart by the Holy Ghost. Accordingly, the Holy Spirit is described (2 Cor. 4 : 13) as "the Spirit of faith," *i. e.*, as the "*Author* of faith." * And faith is distinctly enumerated as one of the "fruits of the Spirit." Will any one presume to argue that while all the other graces enumerated in this bright catalogue (Gal. 5 : 22, 23) are inwrought in the soul by the Holy Spirit, "faith" is not His gift?

Let us hear on this point a well-known writer whose views on "assurance" make him a favorite with the Higher Life School—albeit, as the following extracts will show, he has no sympathy

---

* *Hodge on Corinthians*, in loc.

with their principles. I quote from *Marshall on Sanctification:*

"The faith which philosophers commonly treat of, is only a habit of the understanding whereby we assent to a testimony upon the authority of the testifier. [This is the exact idea of faith presented and defended in the tract above mentioned.] Accordingly, some would have faith in Christ to be no more than a believing the truth of things in religion, upon the authority of Christ testifying them. But the apostle showeth that the faith whereby we are justified, is faith in Christ's blood, (Rom. 3: 24, 25) not only in His authority as a testifier. And though a mere assent to a testimony were a sufficient faith for knowledge of things, which the philosophers aimed at; yet we are to consider that the design of saving faith is, not only to know the truth of Christ and His salvation, testified and promised in the Gospel, but also to apprehend and receive Christ and His salvation, as given by and with the promise. Therefore saving faith must necessarily contain two acts [inseparably joined together], believing the truth of the Gospel, and believing on Christ as promised freely to us in the Gospel for all salvation. By the one it receiveth the means whereby Christ is conveyed to us; by the other, it receiveth Christ Himself and His salvation in the means. And both these acts must be performed heartily, with an unfeigned love to the truth, and a desire of Christ and His salvation above all things."—After referring to faith as "the gift of God," he observes: "For the accomplishing of this great work of our new creation in Christ, the Spirit of God doth first work upon our hearts by and with the Gospel, to produce in us the *grace of faith*. And when saving faith is wrought in us, the same Spirit giveth us fast hold of Christ by it. As He openeth the mouth of faith to receive Christ, so he filleth it with Christ. The same Spirit of Christ doth work saving faith in us, and doth answer the aim and end of that faith, by giving us union and fellowship with Christ by it. We are first passive and then active, in this great work of mystical union; we are first apprehended of Christ, and then we apprehend Christ. Christ entereth *first* into the soul, to join himself to it by giving it the spirit of faith; and so the soul receiveth Christ and His Spirit by their own power; as the sun first enlighteneth our eyes, and then we can see it by its own light. This union is fully accomplished by Christ's giving the spirit of faith to us, even [momentarily] before we act that faith in the reception of Him; because, by this grace or spirit of faith, the soul is inclined and disposed to an active receiving of Christ." "Faith is the uniting grace whereby Christ dwelleth in us, and we in Him; and therefore it is the first grace wrought in our regeneration, and the means of all the rest."

"They that slight the work of faith for its *easiness*, show that they were never yet made sensible of innumerable sins, and the terrible curse of the law and the wrath of God that they lie under; and of the darkness and vanity of their minds, the corruption and hardness of their hearts, and their bondage under the power of sin and Satan; and have not been truly humbled, without which they cannot believe in a right manner. So difficult is this great work, that we cannot possibly perform it until the *Spirit of God work faith in us* by His mighty power." *

These views, which the author fortifies by ample Scripture testimonies, may be usefully contrasted with those previously cited. If, then, faith be a grace, a Divine "gift," it is clearly to be *prayed for*, just as we pray for love, joy, peace, and their kindred virtues. No wonder the writer of the tract felt embarrassed by the appeal

Directions, iv., xii.

of the twelve, "Lord, increase our faith." To allege (as she does) that they erred in this request, is without warrant from the context, and, as may be safely assumed, without the sanction of any recognized Biblical expositor. With as much reason it might be argued, that the poor man erred who cried (Matt. 9 : 24) "Lord, I believe: help thou mine unbelief." Or that Paul erred when he prayed that God would *increase the faith* of the Ephesian and Thessalonian Christians. (Eph. 3 : 14–17; 2 Thess. 1 : 11.) These Christians had faith already, and, according to the new scheme, power to exercise as much more as they wanted. Why pray for that which is "not a grace"? An illustration may help to put this rash and hurtful teaching in its true light. In Jenks's *Prayers*, one of the very best volumes of its class in our language, there is a *"Prayer for Faith and Trust in God,"* a portion of which follows:

"Without faith it is impossible to please thee, O God: and therefore I come to beg of thee that faith which is thy gift. Lord, help my unbelief, and increase my faith. Whatever thou hast revealed, let me take it upon the credit of thy word: and where I have thy promise, let me not stagger through unbelief, but freely persuade myself that it shall be as thou hast said. Oh, bless and enrich my soul with such a holy, lively, and unfeigned faith, as may enlighten my mind and purify my heart, and influence my whole life; such a faith, as may enable me to receive Jesus Christ for my Saviour, and heartily to give up myself to Him as my Lord: that, being ruled and sanctified by Him in this life, I may be for ever saved and glorified by Him in the life that is to come. Oh, help me so to assent unto the truths, that I may also consent to the terms, of the Gospel. And give me that effectual faith which shall work by love; that faith which shall enable me to overcome the world, and to fix my attention on those great and glorious things which are unseen and eternal. . . . Yea, make me so sound and strong in the faith, that my faith may never fail: but that it may be found to praise and honor and glory in every time of trial, and at the great appearing of our Lord and Saviour Jesus Christ. Amen."

If we are to listen to the counsel we are weighing, *this is not a prayer which a Christian ought to offer!* Can such teaching possibly be put forth as drawn from the word of God? or propagated, without doing serious mischief?

It is not the wont of evangelical teachers to disparage faith. They magnify it as a cardinal grace in the whole business of a sinner's salvation, from the moment of his espousals to Christ, to his final preparation for glory. It enters as an essential element into the composition of every other grace, into all faithful working, all patient suffering, and all genuine resignation—into all the hopes, all the victories, and all the joys, of the Christian life. But it is habitually regarded as one of God's gifts. The believer recognizes his dependence upon God, as much for the maintenance and development of his faith, as for his growth in any other grace. He prays as constantly for faith as he does for love and meekness. He is familiar with the promise, "According to your faith, be it unto you:" but it is no part of his creed, that he can exercise faith without the special aid of the Divine Spirit.

It is painfully evident, in so far as the tract alluded to is concerned, that its author does not recognize this truth. It is quite in harmony with the general tone of the tract, that it should contain no acknowledgment whatever of our need of the Spirit's help in order to the exercise of faith— not even in addressing the unconverted. The blessed Paraclete is *not once mentioned*, except in a passage above quoted, *repudiating* the idea that " faith is a gracious disposition of the soul, wrought by the Holy Ghost in answer to prayer."

But for this casual reference, a stranger to Christianity, seeking light as to "*What Faith is and How to exercise it,*" might read this tract through without learning "whether there be any Holy Ghost." It is no apology to say that in others of their publications, all good in man is ascribed to "God's part" in the work of Redemption. Here is a tract on a most important topic, designed for popular circulation, which gives no hint that God has any agency in our exercise of faith; which in fact, offers instructions that are at variance with this sentiment. Such teaching is reprehensible enough when applied to true believers. But what is to be thought of counsel like the following (p. 22), addressed to those who are yet out of Christ?

"The only thing necessary is for us to find out what *is* included in our salvation; and having found it, to dare to reckon it ours *now*. And according to our faith, it shall be unto us. But you may ask, How? I answer, take some declaration of God's. If you are *unconverted*, take His message to sinners in 2 Cor. 5 : 19, for instance, and make up your mind to believe it, irrespective of your feelings, or of your reasonings or of any other thing whatever. Say to yourself, 'God says that He " was in Christ, reconciling the world unto Himself, not imputing their trespasses unto them." I do not see how this can be. I do not feel as if it were so. But God says it, and I know He cannot lie; and I choose to believe Him. He *is* reconciled to me in Christ, and He does not impute my trespasses unto me; I *was* saved through the death of Christ.' Repeat it over and over, putting all the power of will you possess into it. 'I will believe; I choose to believe; I do believe; I am saved.' 'How do you know it?' says Satan; 'do you feel it?' 'No I do not feel it at all; but I know it, because God says so; and I would far rather trust His word than my own feelings, let them be ever so delightful.'"

Here the inquiring sinner is told to disregard alike his "feelings" and the perceptions of his understanding; and, irrespective of his own contrition and of the illumination of the Spirit, to "choose to believe" a Scripture declaration; and thereupon instantly, to *assume*, though without any change of "feeling," that he *is* reconciled to God and saved! If this be so, the "strait gate" is no longer strait. How much better is this teaching than that of the Roman Church, which promises salvation to every one who receives the mass, "irrespective of his feelings," so there be no positive repugnance to the sacrament? Can this grossly unscriptural advice be followed without deadly peril of self-deception?—They go a step beyond this; for besides discountenancing prayer for faith, their books abound with passages which are just what they would have been if it had been an article of their Creed, that God's working in the heart of a disciple is far more dependent upon his faith, than his faith is upon the Spirit's influence. It is not alleged that they believe this: but such is the tone of their writings, and it is only one of various examples in which they divorce what God has united.

We shall see more of this as we proceed; for we are now approaching the core of this remarkable system. "System," it must be called, although its authors disavow all intention of teaching a "doctrine." "This is not a theological book. I frankly confess I have never studied theology, and do not understand its methods nor its terms. . . . Let me beg of the reader not to mind my theological mistakes." "I am not writing to establish a doctrine." "I do not present this secret of the Lord, as a doctrine to be discussed, but as a life to be enjoyed."* It would be a curious problem in psychology, how two intelligent

* R. P. S.; H. W. S.

and conscientious Christians could imagine themselves innocent of setting forth a "doctrine," after writing a half-score of books and pamphlets aimed directly against the current orthodox belief as to sin, holiness, faith, sanctification, and the like; and with the utmost confidence and persistency, essaying to replace that belief with views of their own. They go through the New Testament expounding numerous texts in a way unknown alike to Biblical critics and "ordinary Christians:" but they are "not teaching a doctrine"! It is their mission to reveal the only true method of progress in personal religion—the "*Christian's Secret of a Happy Life*" *—for the sake of which all Christians are pressed to discard their old-time ideas of sanctification: and yet they are "not teaching a doctrine!" Of course these excellent people believe this, or they would not say it. But what impenetrable mists must obscure the celestial atmosphere in which they have their being; and how dimly do they discern either their own condition, or that of their brethren who are slowly toiling upward to the Holy City. They should understand, that no disclaimers of this sort can absolve them from the responsibility of disseminating broad-cast a *scheme of doctrine*

* By H. W. S., *Willard Tract Repository.*

on the vital questions of theology, the truth or falsity of which, as ministering health or contagion to men's souls, *must* be tested by the law and the testimony.

CHAPTER IV.

THE WILL NOT OMNIPOTENT—"CONSE-CRATION."

THE further consideration of their doctrine concerning faith, will make it necessary to notice the irresistible might with which they invest the human *Will*. It were some extenuation of the autocracy ascribed to the will, if it were exerted only for enforcing faith in the verities of Scripture. But the case becomes widely different when it is found that one of the main objects to be received with an implicit faith, is a proposition which *is not laid down in the word of God*, and can be sustained from it, if at all, only by inference and conjecture. This grave charge is as gravely made, and shall be proved.

"How am I to enter into this life of perfect trust? What must I do to secure 'the blessing?' I know it must be in some way by faith; but I have tried to obtain it and *failed*." This state of mind is largely dealt with. Individual cases are cited (it is no marvel they should often occur,) and we have the exact instructions addressed to these perplexed disciples.

"This blessed life is in no sense an attainment but an obtainment. Everything in our salvation is a gift." (Sound doctrine this.) "The soul must be in a receptive attitude. He bestows it only upon the fully-consecrated soul, and it is to be received by faith. Consecration is the first thing. Not in any legal sense, not in order to purchase or deserve the blessing, but to remove the difficulties out of the way and make it possible for God to bestow it (!)" "In order to enter into this blessed interior life of rest and triumph, you have two steps to take. First, entire abandonment; and, second, absolute faith."—What an inversion is here: full consecration as the *prelude* to faith! And in harmony with this arrangement, we have a Chapter on "Consecration" *followed* by a Chapter on "Faith." Was there ever an example of consecration without faith? Is such a thing possible?

Again: "You know in your very soul, that Jesus is able and willing to deliver you. Then commit your case to Him in an absolute abandonment, and believe [here comes in the new object of faith,] that He undertakes it; and at once, knowing what He is and what He has said, claim that He *does* even now fully save. Believe that He (now) delivers *you* from the power of sin, *because He says so."*

A difficulty arises. The seeker after holiness endeavors to consecrate himself. "He has done it, as he thinks; and yet does not feel differently from before: nothing seems changed, as he has been led to expect it would be, and he is completely baffled, and asks the question almost despairingly, 'How am I to know when I am consecrated?' Through a grand device of Satan, the soul cannot believe it is consecrated until it *feels* that it is; and because it does not feel that God has taken it in hand, it cannot believe that He has. As usual, it puts feeling first and faith second. Now God's invariable rule is, faith first and feeling second in everything. . . . To meet this device, you must put faith before feeling. Give yourself to the Lord definitely and fully [what, without 'feeling?'] according to your present light, asking the Holy Spirit to show you all that is contrary to God in your heart or life. If He shows you anything, give it to the Lord immediately, and say in reference to it, 'Thy will be done.' If He shows you nothing, then you must believe that there is nothing, and must conclude that you have given Him all. Then you must believe that He takes you. You positively must not wait to *feel* either that you have given yourself or that He has taken you. You must simply believe it, and reckon it to be the case. . . . You must never even so much as listen to a suggestion to the contrary. If the temptation comes to wonder whether you really have completely surrendered yourself, meet it with an *assertion* that you have. Do not even argue the matter. Repel any such idea instantly and with decision. You meant it then, you mean it now, you have really done it. Your emotions may clamor against the surrender, but your will must hold firm. It is your purpose God looks at, not your feelings about that purpose; and your purpose or will is therefore the only thing you need attend to."

In this mass of crudities, so eminently fitted to mislead the persons it was designed to help, several things are worthy of note. (1) It is sadly overlooked, that "the heart is deceitful above all things." (2) It is assumed, in the face of Scripture and all Christian experience, that true faith may be exercised without any right feeling. But what saith the Scripture? "If thou believest with all thine *heart*." "With the *heart* man believeth unto righteousness." If God regards only the naked "purpose," what means the averment, that "*love* is the fulfilling of the law"? Can I consecrate myself to God without love? Can I, without love, say, "Thy will be done"? (3) While feeling is of no account in judging of one's "consecration," a moment after it is called to play a most important part. You are, with the aid of the Spirit, to search your "heart," and see if there be anything wrong there; in other words, whether there be anything amiss either in your views or your affections, *i. e.*, your *feelings;* and further progress is blocked until this point is settled. So that, after all, the "emotions" are of some account. (4) It is assumed, on the one hand, that the subject of these exercises cannot err in deciding whether his heart and life are in exact accord with the Divine will; and on the other, that God is bound to answer his prayer at once, and in the precise way in which he seeks for guidance. (5) He is to scorn the suggestion as from Satan, albeit confirmed by his own "emotions," that, possibly, he may be mistaken in supposing that his consecration is complete, and, as such, is owned and ratified of God. To any incipient misgiving of this sort rising in his breast, he is to say, "Get thee behind me, Satan." And what if, after all his self-confidence, the rising doubt should happen to be from the Holy Spirit! Is it a thing unheard of that even a saint may deceive himself as to the real character of his exercises, and that the Spirit may show him his error?

In further unfolding the duty and method of that consecration which puts us in a position "where God will *consent* to work in us the good pleasure of His will," we are told: "The life hid with Christ in God is not to be lived in the emotions at all, but in the will; and therefore the varying states of emotion do not in the least disturb or affect the reality of the life, if only the will is kept steadfastly abiding in its centre, God's will. . . . It is sometimes thought that the emotions are the governing power in our nature. But as a matter of practical experience, I think we all of us know that there is something within us behind our emotions and behind our wishes—an independent self—that after all decides everything and controls everything. Our emotions belong to us, and are suffered and enjoyed by us, but they are not ourselves; and if God is to take possession of us, it must be into this central will or personality that He shall enter. . . . The moment we see that the will is king, we shall utterly disregard anything that clamors against it, and shall claim as real its decisions, let the emotions rebel as they may." A young man struggling to obtain "the blessing" and discouraged, was told this blessed secret concerning the will: that if he would only put his will over on to the believing side; if he would choose to believe; if in short he would, in the Ego of his nature, say, "I will believe! I do believe!" he need not trouble about his emotions, for they would find themselves compelled, sooner or later, to come into harmony. "What," he said, "do you mean to tell me that I can *choose* to believe in that way when nothing seems true to me, and will that kind of believing be real?" "Yes," was the answer: "your part is only this—to *put your will over on God's side* [the favorite formula] in this matter of believing: and when you do this, God immediately takes possession of it, and works in you to will and to do of His good pleasure, and you will soon find that He has brought all the rest of your nature into subjection to Himself." The young man thereupon said, "I can give my will to God, and I do." And thenceforth his life became one of unintermitted joy and triumph.

After citing some other examples, the book proceeds, in iteration of the same doctrine: "Is your will put into God's hands? Does your will decide to believe? Does your will choose to obey? If this is the case, then you *are* in the Lord's hands, and you decide to believe, and you choose to obey; for your will is yourself. And the thing is done. The transaction with God is as real, where only your will acts, as where every emotion coincides. It does not seem real to you; but in God's sight it is as real. [How do you know this?] . . . When then this feeling of unreality or hypocrisy comes, do not be troubled by it. It is only in your emotions and is not worth a moment's thought. . . . If your will is on God's side, you are no hypocrite at this moment in claiming as your own the blessed reality of belonging altogether to Him, even though your emotions may all declare the contrary."

Both the philosophy and the theology of these extracts are passing wonderful. To deal with them in detail, were quite impracticable. But there are certain things which must be noticed.

(1) In what sense does the author use the words, "will," and "emotions"? Whatever the sense, these terms are evidently designed to include the whole mental and moral man. What is not in the will, is in the emotions, and *vice versâ*. Now there are two senses, a narrower and a broader, in which will is used, alike by peasants and sages. In the former, it indicates simply the faculty of

self-determination; the power by which we choose and refuse. In the latter, it comprehends, together with this faculty, all the desires, affections, and emotions. Everything depends upon the sense in which the word is employed. The writer under review says, "By the will, I do not mean the wish of the man, nor even his purpose, but the choice, the deciding power, the king, to which all that is in the man must yield obedience. It is the man in short—the 'Ego'—that which we feel to be ourselves." On the next page (see above) the "Ego," is distinctly affirmed to be the will in its restricted sense—the power of choosing. This is clearly the usage of the word throughout. In its wider sense, as embracing the affections and everything within us except the power of volition, these passages would have no meaning. To choose holiness would be the same as having holiness. To choose Christ as our sanctification, would be the same as already having Him in that capacity: for the very act of choice implies the right apprehension of His character, supreme love to Him, and trust in Him, as the Fountain of life and strength and holiness. But the state of mind with which the author deals, is very different from this. Both the emotions and the understanding are arrayed against the will,—which shows plainly that the will is used in its limited sense. It can be only the understanding which says, "Nothing seems *true* to me." And the emotions "clamor" against the wise and just volition which would lead them captive.

(2) The marvellous postulate is assumed here, that a *simple volition*, if repeated again and again, *can control the desires and affections*—for these must be included in the "emotions," otherwise they have no place at all in the work of perfect consecration. Now, in view of the reiterated statement, that the will "lies behind our emotions and behind our wishes," and, enthroned in that innermost shrine of our being, wields an imperial sceptre over the entire man, it might be pertinent to ask, whether it really does exercise this unchallenged sovereignty. Does it act without consulting the desires? Do you choose that for which you have no desire? Have liking and disliking, inclination and aversion, nothing to do with your volitions? And if the truth really be, that the will is, not in rare instances, but ordinarily, the *servant* of desire, what becomes of its crown and sceptre?

In this scheme, "volition is king." It has only to choose God as its holiness, and the vagrant, lawless affections will be "compelled" to fall in. This is saying, that we can love by choosing to love; or hate by choosing to hate. You *will* to believe: and thereupon you do believe, and your love, tied to your will as a slave tied to his overseer, presently follows its master and rejoices in God. The common doctrine is, that the Divine Spirit illumines the mind to discern, more and more, the excellency and glory of the Redeemer, enkindles an ardent desire to be His and to be like Him, and puts a gentle and loving constraint upon the *will,* so that it chooses Him as its Saviour and Portion, its all in all. These exercises are all to be ascribed to the Spirit's agency, and they are virtually simultaneous. The naked volition does not go out alone toward Christ, and command its reluctant vassals, the affections, to follow after. If they had not already, under a very different Leader, found their way to the cross, no mere volition, however peremptory, could bring them there,—for, I repeat it, you cannot love by merely *willing* to love, nor (let me add) can you believe by willing to believe. I stood by the bedside of one of the most cultured men I have known, whose whole being was engrossed with the question of his salvation; and with the deepest emotion he said to me, "I would give the world to be able to believe as you believe." Here was a *will* to believe, what could it accomplish?—Again, I visited through a protracted and fatal illness, a man equally distinguished as a profound jurist and an acute metaphysician—the author, indeed, of an able work on *The Will*. His illness found him without the only armor which could carry him safely through the last conflict. It was a conscious want. His agitation and distress almost unnerved me. Day after day, as I pointed him to the Lamb of God, he would exclaim in anguish of spirit, "Oh, for *faith—for faith!* Give me faith! Give me faith!" This man of might, who had studied the abstruse problems of the will for a score or two of years, knew too much of the constitution of the human mind to imagine that crying, "I *will* believe! I *do* believe!" would beget the faith for which he was yearning. And like thousands of others, on the approach of death, he *prayed* importunately for that faith which God alone could give him. It is my humble belief, that in the case of both these eminent men, their supplications were answered. Nor can I forbear to add, that had I addressed them in the terms prescribed in the tract on "Faith" and others of these publications, they would justly have treated it as a mockery.

Equally certain is it, that you cannot order your "emotions," *i. e.* your desires and affections, this and that way, at your will. As over against the dogmatic teachings of these books, we may cite the experience of an apostle. "To *will* is present with me, but how to perform that which is good I find not." (Rom. 7 : 18.) Even in the 'Seventh of Romans' St. Paul may, perhaps, be allowed to testify as to the alleged regal power of the will. And we have his authority here for asserting, that the emotions and affections do not obey a determination of the will. If the response comes, as it probably will, "The apostle said this before he was delivered from his conflict with indwelling sin:" it may be pertinent to ask, was he not, at this period, at least as far on in the Christian life as those very imperfect believers to whom you are constantly saying, "You have only to will to believe, and your refractory emotions will strike their flag and obey the august volition"? Can their volitions do what even Paul's desires could not? If any one still hesitates on this point, let him try the experiment, whether he can love a person by willing to love him. "We may will with all our energy to love an object now odious, and our will produces no manner of effect, except to show us our inability to change our affections by the force of the will. On the contrary, we find by experience that our volitions are influenced constantly by our prevailing desires. *No man ever put forth a volition which was not the effect of some desire, feeling, or inclination.*" * Or, as Vinet puts it: "We must *first* of all love God, which *depends not on our will;* because we cannot love an object in which we do not find our happiness." So much for volition being "king!"

* Archibald Alexander, D. D.

CHAPTER V.

FURTHER MISTAKES AS TO FAITH AND CONSECRATION.

Having performed the act of consecration, what is it I am now to believe? Is it a distinct statement of the Scriptures, or is it something which I *infer* to be true? The quotations already made answer this question. What you are to believe is (you are told), that you *are* freed from your body of death; that you *are* "dead to sin;" that your consecration is complete. "Repel instantly any temptation to doubt on this point. Do not even argue the matter. *God has said it*; and to doubt of it, is to dishonor Him. If you are in Christ, the body of sin, the very source and centre of sin, *is* destroyed, not by any daily dying of your own, not by any mortifying of this lust or the other, but by the death of Christ. . . . The last necessary step to take, then, in order to enter into God's way of holiness, is to take God at His word in this matter, as you did in the matter of justification, and to believe that you are dead to sin because He says it. You must not wait for signs of death, or for a feeling of death, before you believe; but you must believe it on the authority of God, although to your own consciousness, *sin may seem to be more vigorous and outbreaking than ever.* (!) —You must go to Him and say 'Lord Jesus, I am dead to sin. I died in Thee, and therefore I *am* dead. I could not believe it, if Thou hadst not said it, for the evidence of my own senses tells me exactly the opposite. But *Thou hast said it*, and therefore I believe it. I am dead to sin because I am in Thee.'" *

That a full assurance of faith and hope is ordinarily attainable by believers, has been already stated. Many a Christian is able to say, "I *know* whom I have believed." Of the Scriptural method of attaining to this happy estate it must suffice for the present to say, that it usually comes from comparing the fruits and effects of our faith with the word of God. The Bible is the seal. We are the wax. Does the impression correspond with the seal? Do we discern there, love, humility, obedience, hatred of sin, longing after holiness, supreme devotion to Christ? The Holy Spirit has in His word specified these and

* *God's Way of Holiness*, II. W. S., Appendix.

other marks of a gracious state. He implants the corresponding graces in the heart of the believer, and enabling him to perceive their agreement, thus witnesses with his own spirit that he is born again. Doubtless the blessed Spirit sometimes gives this attestation in a more direct way, and even at the moment of conversion. We may not limit the Holy One of Israel. But ordinarily full assurance is a plant of not very rapid growth; the rich inheritance of believers who have long been planted in the house of the Lord, and are so covered with the fruits of righteousness that every eye recognizes the lovely garniture, and every tongue, except their own, extols it.

By no such circuitous and wearisome process is full assurance reached, according to the Higher Life theology. In no other school claiming to be evangelical, would it be deemed proper, or warrantable, or safe, to say to any human being, whatever his protestations and professions of piety, " You are bound to believe yourself a child of God and fully consecrated to His service, *allhough you are conscious that your sin may be more vigorous and outbreaking than ever.*" Is not this the rankest Antinomianism? And is it not putting men's souls in fearful peril, to scatter such sentiments broad-cast among the people?

This absolute assurance, we are told, comes at once. It is unhappily based upon the belief of a proposition which is derived from Scripture only by inference—an inference which may prove to be chimerical. The fallacy which runs through these essays, is that of confounding two very distinct statements, as will be made apparent by the following syllogism. (1) He that believeth in Christ, shall be saved. (2) I do believe in Christ. (3) Therefore I am saved. For the major term of this syllogism, you have the authority of Scripture. For the minor you have not. The Bible nowhere tells you in direct terms, that *you* are a believer. It points out the characteristics of a believer. It offers you Divine help in ascertaining whether you are in Christ. You may have valid grounds for believing that you are. But this conviction must perforce be based upon your reasoning, not upon any "Thus saith the Lord." In believing or trusting in Christ, you are looking out of yourself to the Saviour. To *know* whether you do really trust in Him, involves a reflex act of the mind—a looking into your own heart. I cannot possibly doubt that Christ will receive whoever comes to Him: for He has said it. I *may* doubt whether *I* have come to Him. I think I have. So far as my own consciousness goes, I believe I have. But He has not said this in so many words, and I am not sure of it. Multitudes have deceived themselves on this point, who have had a confident persuasion of their having embraced Christ: some who could even say, "In Thy name have we cast out devils." Is there no possibility that you or I may be misled by a treacherous heart?

As this pertains to the very marrow of the scheme, and is, in a sort, the hinge upon which the whole structure swings, it may crave further scrutiny. The consecrating act, according to these teachers, marks the crisis of your history. It carries you over from a state of bondage, to a state of freedom; out of a dismal life of toil, and discouragement, and uncertainty, into one of rest, and joy, and assurance; from a condition in which you sin, more or less, by transgression or omission, every day, to one in which you do not consciously sin at all. Whether this mighty transition be held up by the sacred writers with the prominence which might seem due to its pre-eminent importance, is a point that will be adverted to hereafter. For the present, let it suffice to say, that it is here resolved into an exercise of faith (with or without "feeling," as the case may be) in respect to two propositions neither of which can be quoted by you in the words of the Holy Ghost. One of these propositions is, that having, according to the best of your knowledge and ability, performed this act of consecration, you are *now* "dead to sin;" and must *believe* this, though your bosom be filled with misgivings, and your sins appear to you to be in full activity. The other proposition is, that to be "dead to sin," is to have entered upon an *unsinning life*. What this phrase really means, is a question upon which Biblical critics may and do differ. But no one will pretend that the Holy Ghost has explicitly taught, that it is synonymous with a state of perfect holiness. This construction may be put upon it by those who have a theory to support. But where our salvation is concerned, we do not want deductions and conjectures. We must have the express language of the unerring word. And we urge it as a cardinal objection to the Higher Life school, that they require us, as the indispensable condition of obtaining "the blessing," to believe without wavering, propositions which are destitute of any direct Scriptural authority. Not only are Christians exhorted to build upon this precarious foundation, but they are warned against any distrust of the faith they suppose themselves to have exercised. This consecrating faith, their books tell us, is often the result of a long and violent inward conflict. All the powers and susceptibilities of the soul are engrossed with it. And yet an act of faith put forth amidst this turmoil of feeling—an act, according to their scheme, of tremendous and far-reaching efficacy—is not for a moment to be challenged. Any suspicion of its reality is to be hooted away as coming from the father of lies.— In all seriousness it may be asked, do these teachers regard it as so simple a matter to learn the quality of our own moral exercises, that they feel free to say to inquirers of whatever type, and especially to those who are wrought up at the moment to the highest pitch of excitement, "Do not doubt as to your faith: do not reason about it. Say 'I have done it;' and then take it for granted that it *is* done; and that you have God's authority for it." Unless I am incapable, after long study, of understanding these writers, this is precisely what they teach. And it cannot fail to awaken equal amazement and regret, on the part of any who consider the fatal facility with which men embrace delusive hopes in religion, that lessons like these should be addressed to promiscuous crowds, and widely diffused through the press.

A word just here by way of Postscript to the preceding paragraph. A week after it was written, having occasion to consult "*Edwards on the Affections*," the following passage met my eye:—"There are those who mean by faith, believing with confidence that they are in a good state. But whence do they learn this? If this is faith, the Pharisees had faith in an eminent degree; some of whom, Christ assures us, committed the unpardonable sin against the Holy Ghost. The Scriptures represent faith as that by which men are brought *into* a good state; and therefore it cannot be the same thing as believing that they *are already* in a good state. To suppose that faith consists in believing that we are spiritually safe, is in effect the same thing as to suppose that faith consists in believing that we have faith, or in *believing that we believe*." It is curious and significant that President Edwards should here have hit upon the precise formula which is so much in vogue with the Higher Life writers.

CHAPTER VI.

NOVELTIES IN SCRIPTURE-INTERPRETATION —MYSTICISM.

We find the believer now in possession of Christ as his complete sanctification. What this means precisely in the scheme under review, it is not very easy to learn. We are told that " Christ is *our own holiness* just as really and fully as He is our own sacrifice for sin." * Your new life is a life of perfect repose. There must be no " straining and striving" after growth. Your whole function consists in lying passively in Christ's hands, careful only that no unbelief springs up to arrest His working within you. Now that I am in Christ, I have done working. I roll upon Him all the responsibility † of repelling my temptations, holding in chains those lower appetites which I have in entire subjection, and keeping alive my graces.

* W. E. Boardman.

† This is the traditional resource of the evangelists of Perfectionism:—" We roll the responsibility of our future and eternal obedience, upon the Everlasting Arm."

The striving, the wrestling, the fighting, are all His. And if the work be His, *the responsibility is His*, and there is no room left for me to worry about it. Christ does it all. In support of views of this sort, they quote such texts as the following: "I am crucified with Christ; nevertheless I live; yet not I, but Christ liveth in me; and the life which I now live in the flesh, I live by the faith of the Son of God, who loved me and gave Himself for me." "Christ in you the hope of glory." "Likewise reckon ye also yourselves to be dead indeed unto sin, but alive unto God through Jesus Christ our Lord." "If Christ be in you, the body is dead because of sin; but the Spirit is life because of righteousness." This class of texts is interpreted as proving that the "consecrated" believer lives without sin, by reason of Christ having taken such plenary possession of him that He now lives his life for him.

Very much of the language employed on this subject, affiliates the theory with the radical idea of Mysticism, the deification of man's nature. "The essential union is the spiritual marriage where there is a communication of substance, when God takes the soul for His spouse, unites it to Himself, not personally, nor by any act or means, but immediately reducing all to a unity. The soul ought not, nor can, any more make any distinction between God and itself. God is the soul, the soul is God."*—Those of the Mystics, who stop short of this extreme, teach, in keeping with it, that perfect holiness is to be attained by devout contemplation, almost to the exclusion of outward ordinances, theological study, and Christian activity. Knowledge, purity, strength, growth, come, not so much through prayer and the actings of a lively faith upon the truths of God's word, as by simply yielding the soul without effort to the Divine influence. As the legitimate fruit of this principle, the Church has been disfigured and corroded by asceticism in its various forms of monkery, pilgrimages, and hermit-life.

Without attempting to homologate the Higher Life system with that of Madame Guyon and Molinos and their followers, we find at its core the same principle of passivity, and the same style of phraseology,—as if holiness were, so to speak, poured into the quiescent soul, as wine into a vase. They differ, however, from other schools of Perfectionists, in assigning this potential agency officially to the Second Person of the Trinity. That Christ dwells in the heart of every believer, is part of the universal faith of evangelical Chris-

* Madame Guyon.

tendom. And every true believer takes Christ as his sanctification. This indwelling of Christ, as already observed, is the indwelling of His Spirit. "If any man have not the *Spirit* of Christ, he is none of His. And if *Christ* be in you (using the names interchangeably) the body is dead because of sin." "If ye through the Spirit do mortify the deeds of the body, ye shall live: for as many as are led by the Spirit of God they are the sons of God." "It is expedient for you that I go away; for if I go not away, the Comforter will not come unto you; but if I depart I will send Him unto you." "I will pray the Father, and He shall give you another Comforter, that He may *abide* with you for ever, even the Spirit of truth." "He shall glorify me; for He shall receive of mine, and shall show it unto you." Comparing these passages (and the New Testament is full of them) with those which represent Christ as dwelling in His people, it is evident that *He dwells in them by His Holy Spirit.* This is the usual mode of stating the doctrine. It is so interwoven with the current language of the pulpit, the prayer-meeting, the familiar intercourse of Christians, and the whole body of Scriptural literature, that to multiply texts in proof of it would be a work of supererogation.

And yet in this whole series of books and tracts, the cardinal doctrine of which is the indwelling of Christ in the believer, its laws, its fruits, its priceless joys, and how it is to be maintained, I have not met with the formal statement *in a single instance*, that "Christ dwells in the believer by His Holy Spirit." They may believe this. They may indirectly teach it. But in these treatises, where, if anywhere, it is vitally needed, one sadly misses that specific expression of the idea, which gives tone and complexion to all the standard sermons and essays on Sanctification.

Another omission is still more significant. There is one passage in which our Saviour speaks directly of the sanctification of His people. It is the sole instance in which He uses the word in respect to them, and is impressed with all the solemnity which attaches to His parting prayer. It is probably the sentence which first occurs to the mind of nearly every Christian on hearing, from whatever lips, the word "Sanctify." It is clothed with an exceptional importance even as among the Messiah's utterances, because it indicates the *means* of sanctification. On every ground it is entitled to the most devout and earnest consideration on the part of all who bear His name and would bear His image. That it should escape the notice of any intelligent preacher or writer on this subject, is simply incredible. If it is not quoted and commented on, this must be of forethought and design. Here is the passage:—"*Sanctify them through Thy truth: Thy word is truth. As Thou hast sent me into the world, even so have I also sent them into the world. And for their sakes I sanctify myself, that they also might be sanctified through the truth.*" (John 17 : 17–19.) Will it be believed that the Higher Life writers never quote this passage? I say, "never." In their four largest volumes,* devoted to an elaborate exposition of Sanctification, this memorable prayer of our Great High Priest does not once occur; nor have I seen it in any of their tracts which have fallen in my way. It is too plain to admit of controversy, that they are not drawn to the passage. It is not to their liking. It speaks emphatically and by iteration of the TRUTH as the *instrumental means* of sanctification; a sentiment which does not coalesce with their favorite theory, to wit: that the indwelling Christ "*is* the believer's holiness," and that all his progress depends upon his quiescently

---

* *The Higher Christian Life*, W. E. Boardman; *Holiness through Faith*, R. P. S.; *Walking in the Light*, R. P. S.; *The Christian's Secret of a Happy Life*, H. W. S.

resting there, and "not hindering" Christ from doing His work in and for him.

The writer confesses his inability to fathom the import of this phraseology, which pervades all their writings. The doctrine of the Mystics, that the soul is re-absorbed into the Divine essence, however visionary, is at least intelligible. The common orthodox doctrine, that Christ, the Head of His body the Church, dwells in His members by the Holy Spirit, who sanctifies them through the truth, is no less intelligible. As neither of these appears to be their doctrine, there would seem to be no hypothesis left but the gross one, of the actual *Personality* of the God-man, Christ Jesus, who lived and taught and suffered in Judea, entering into, and, in a sort, supplanting, the personality of the believer. It is not charged that they hold this novel type of Transubstantiation. All that is alleged, is, that if they did hold it, they would find the language they now use well fitted to express it. Look, for example, at the case which is cited as furnishing a "splendid illustration" of their views. The author of the book visits an "Idiot Asylum." The patients, going through an exercise with dumb-bells, "made all sorts of awkward movements, out of harmony with the music. One little girl, however, made perfect movements. Not a jar nor a break disturbed the harmony of her exercises. And the reason was, not that she had more strength than the others, but that she had no strength at all. She could not so much as close her hands over the dumb-bells, nor lift her arms, and the master had to stand behind her and do it all. She yielded up her members as instruments to him, and his strength was made perfect in her weakness. The yielding was her part; the responsibility was all his." This is a " picture of the Christian life. . . . Who, then, would not glory in being so utterly weak and helpless, that the Lord Jesus Christ should find no hinderance to the perfect working of His mighty power through us and in us?" *

If this meant only what the apostle means when he speaks of God as " working in us," or when he says, " When I am weak, then am I strong," the lesson would command instant and general assent. But as interpreted by scores of other passages, it must be taken to signify something quite different from the accepted doctrine of the oneness of Christ and His people. Whether so intended or not, unbiased readers will understand this strain of assertion and illustration, as importing that the believer, on attaining his " con-

* *The Christian's Secret.*

secration," lapses into the condition of an automaton. We readily grant that there is much about the union between our blessed Lord and His disciples, which must remain a mystery to us in our present imperfect state. But, assured that He is still God and man in one Person, and that His bodily presence is now not on earth but in heaven, we can conceive of no sense in which the Personality of His twofold nature enters subjectively into the person of the believer, and, to all intents and purposes, absorbs the latter into itself. Not only does this notion clothe the Saviour's Mediatorial *body* with ubiquity, but it reduces the child of God to a mere machine, and, in set terms often repeated, encourages him to believe that he is no longer "responsible" for the working, the fighting, the conquering, to which the Master constantly exhorts him. Whereas on the Scriptural plan, of Christ dwelling in the disciple by the Holy Spirit, and thus nourishing his faith and all other graces through the truth, everything becomes lucid, harmonious, animating, and eminently practical.

If it be so, that the holiness of Christ literally "becomes the holiness of His people," as these writers teach, then their theory of sanctification instead of going too far, does not go far enough. What they claim is "freedom from *conscious* sin." The Saviour was absolutely sinless; and they are inconsistent in challenging for themselves anything less. Not to dwell upon this, the text from which their favorite doctrine takes its designation, is, 1 Cor. 1 : 30 : "But of Him are ye in Christ Jesus, who of God is made unto us wisdom, and righteousness, and sanctification, and redemption." By the righteousness of Christ here is usually understood the righteousness by which a sinner is justified : by redemption, his final and complete deliverance from all evil. Now as to the two remaining terms, it is purely arbitrary to distinguish them after the fashion of these expositors. If the "sanctification" be perfect, is the "wisdom" imperfect? You have precisely the same authority for claiming to be *perfect in wisdom*, on accepting Christ, that you have for claiming to be perfect in sanctification. Christ is perfect wisdom, the very "wisdom of God," and you take Him as your wisdom. Why do you shrink from asserting that you are now faultless in your wisdom? It were a more modest pretension than that you are faultless in your holiness. But the delusion would be too glaring : neither your own eyes nor those of others could endure it. Whereas the "ordinary Christian" has no embarrassment in appropriating the

Saviour to himself as He is here set forth. He embraces Him not only as his perfect righteousness and his perfect redemption, but as his perfect wisdom and his perfect sanctification. Both he finds in Christ. He is the Light of the world. He alone reveals the Father. By His word and Spirit, He reveals to His Church the whole will of God in all things concerning their edification and salvation. Himself the Truth, He guides His people into the truth, and leads them on, from stage to stage, in their knowledge of Divine things. This gradual process will have its consummation when the believer no longer "sees through a glass darkly," but sees His Redeemer "face to face." Then he will, according to the capacity of a creature, be "perfect" in wisdom. The sponsors of the new doctrine will doubtless concur in this view. And it is submitted, that by any fair principle of exegesis, the same view must be taken of the cognate term, sanctification. It is a gradual work, and will surely reach its perfection, but only when the pilgrim reaches his heavenly home: his wisdom and his sanctification will be perfected at one and the same moment.

But we are not left to any conjectural interpretation of this phrase. The position taken is this: The apostle affirms that Christ is our sanctification: therefore, on receiving Him as such, our sanctification must needs be complete. If this be true of us, it must *a fortiori* have been true of those to whom he directly addressed the language; and of whom he says in the same verse, "ye are in Christ Jesus." What proof, then, have we that *these Corinthians* had attained (or "obtained," as we are admonished to say,) the Higher Life plane of holiness? The sort of proof which we have, is supplied in this same chapter: "I thank my God always on your behalf for the grace of God which is given you by Jesus Christ; that in everything ye are enriched by Him in all utterance and in all knowledge; even as the testimony of Christ was confirmed in you: so that ye come behind in no gift, waiting for the coming of our Lord Jesus Christ, who shall confirm you unto the end, that ye may be blameless in the day of our Lord Jesus Christ." (1 Cor. 1: 4–8.) This is a far stronger Higher Life passage than the verse we have been considering. Surely *these* Christians must have got beyond the infection of " known sin." Alas, for human inventions! For only two verses afterward, the apostle brushes away all such cobwebs, on this wise:—" It hath been declared unto me of you, my brethren, by them which are of the house of Chloe, that there are contentions among you. . . . One saith, I am of Paul; and I, of Apollos; and I, of Cephas; and I, of Christ." And again (Chapt. 3 : 1–3.) "For ye are yet carnal: for whereas there is among you envying, and strife, and divisions, are ye not yet carnal, and walk as men?" Sorry specimens these of "perfect" Christians! Yet, nevertheless, they are the same persons who have "taken Christ as their sanctification," and whom he so commends for their graces. The obvious explanation is, that they were true believers, but still beset with infirmities and sins. He ascribes to them, as is his usual custom, gracious affections and the exalted prospects which are the heritage of all renewed sinners, not because they have "attained," but because the germs of the new spiritual creation are deposited in their breasts, and, *potentially*, not only the blade, but the ear, and the full corn in the ear, are there. But the ripened grain is "not yet"—and will not be until the harvest.—Can these apparently discordant passages be harmonized on the principles of the new Perfectionism?

Another favorite text which is wrested in a similar way from its true import, is that one so precious to every child of God: "For ye are dead (*ye died*),* and your life is hid with Christ in

* "*Ye are dead.*" Some eminent commentators take this

God." (Col. 3 : 3.) This imports, it is claimed, in both its clauses, the perfect sanctification of the "consecrated" believer. Let us see. Suppose a company of Higher Life disciples assembled, all of whom profess to have obtained "the blessing," and some Christian Minister should come in and address them as follows: "My friends, set your affection on things above, not on things on the earth. Mortify your members which are upon the earth, fornication, uncleanness, inordinate affection, evil concupiscence, and covetousness, which is idolatry. . . . Put off all anger, wrath, malice, blasphemy, filthy communication out of your mouth. Lie not one to another, seeing that ye have put off the old man and have put on the new man." Can it be doubted, that every face would put on a look of blended amaze-

phrase wherever it occurs, not in a moral but a judicial sense. Does it not really include both? By reason of your oneness with Christ, when He died, ye died. Ye are absolved from the penal curse. And the life which you now live, is a life from and in Him, who, having died for our offences, rose again for our justification, and became the Fountain of life to all his people.

> "O Lamb of God, who once wast slain,
> We thank Thee for that bitter pain:
> Let us partake Thy death, that we
> May enter into life with Thee."

ment and incredulity, on hearing such exhortations addressed to *them?* that one would say to another, "This good man means well, but he has mistaken his audience. He is not aware that we have gone up to a higher plane: that we are 'dead to sin, and our life is hid with Christ in God;' and therefore we have no occasion to be warned against these carnal appetites and habits which we have so happily subjugated." And yet this is the precise language the apostle employs in the immediate context. In one and the same breath he tells the Colossians, "Ye are dead and your life is hid with Christ in God; therefore mortify your members" etc. It is clear to demonstration, that in St. Paul's judgment, it is far from being any evidence of a sinless state, that one "is dead, and has his life hid with Christ in God." What he means, is, that the Christian is "dead" because he died to the law with Christ, and has received the *principle* of a new life; indwelling sin no more *reigns* over him; the death of the old man, his corrupt nature, is designed and begun, and will in the end certainly be accomplished—just as a condemned criminal is a dead man, though his execution be delayed; and meanwhile, the fresh life which animates him and which has its hidden springs in Christ, will go on increasing in strength and symmetry till it reaches its full maturity in a better clime.

These writers, again, are fond of quoting Galatians 2 : 20. In the preceding verse the apostle says: "I through the law am dead to the law, that I might live unto God." As if he had said: "The law itself, revealing to me the corruption of my heart and the sin that taints all I do, has slain my former hopes and made me dead to all thought of seeking justification by my own works. Nevertheless, while abandoning the law as a covenant of works, I am not without the law as a rule of duty, for the Gospel which I have embraced, binds me to that supreme and perfect love to God which is the first and great commandment, and, in truth, includes all the rest." Then, describing this new life which has superseded his old life of legality, he says: "I am crucified with Christ: nevertheless I live, yet not I, but Christ liveth in me; and the life which I now live in the flesh, I live by the faith of the Son of God, who loved me and gave Himself for me."—"I am crucified with Christ." In virtue of the indissoluble union between Christ and His people, when He died, they died. Through their participation in His death, they are delivered from the fatal bondage of sin and death : the old man is destroyed. "Nevertheless I live, yet not I, but Christ liveth in me." As they died with Christ, so they live with Him. His life is the source and support of their life. So exclusively do they derive their new life from Him, that it is rather He who lives than themselves. Yet the apostle, as if designing to interdict the very error of the Higher Life School, immediately explains what he means by the Saviour's living the Christian's life for him. "The life which I now live in the flesh [the life 'which Christ liveth in me'] I live *by the faith of the Son of God.*" It is not that the *Person* of Christ dwells in the believer; but, the believer trusting in His all-sufficient merits—relying on His atoning death, and accepting Him as his all in all—the Saviour abides in him *by His Spirit and word*, and enables him to live a life of faith upon the Son of God. That this is the import of the passage, is apparent from its harmony with the current teaching of the New Testament respecting the relation between Christ and His people.

CHAPTER VII.

MORE TEXTS MISINTERPRETED—ROMANS VII.

A THIRD class of texts relied upon as one of the buttresses of the new system, is made up of the promises of God to redeem Israel from all iniquity: and of these, the choice one is, 1 John 1:7: "The blood of Jesus Christ His Son cleanseth us from all sin." This means, we are told many times over, that the believer is cleansed *now* ("cleanseth")—not partially, but wholly, "from *all* sin." How perplexing it is to attempt to make this interpretation blend with the context, may be seen by referring to "*Holiness through Faith*," pp. 74, 75. As the passage is clearly fatal to the whole scheme, and will be noticed hereafter, it must suffice to indicate here what is involved in the exposition just cited. The venerable apostle is speaking, throughout the whole Epistle, of sincere believers. If this verse is to be taken, as they tell us, in its literal import, it teaches, (1) that *all* Christians are cleansed. (2) That they are cleansed from *all* sin. And (3) that they are cleansed from all sin *now*,—not merely from what they may to-day see to be sin in themselves, but from all that God sees to be sin in them. In other words, all true Christians are *absolutely sinless.* You must either accept this interpretation, or you must limit and qualify the meaning—a liberty which you deny to others, unless they are ready to qualify it in your way. On the fundamental principle, that all texts are to be interpreted according to the analogy of faith, each to be explained by other texts, so as to make a consistent whole, there is no difficulty in ascertaining the apostle's meaning here. He speaks for the entire Christian brotherhood when he refers to the blood of Christ as the great, and, in a sense, the only purifier from sin. What resource is there for the convinced sinner—what for the believer day by day through his pilgrimage—but the precious blood of Christ? Nor is its virtue either restricted to sins of a certain hue, or efficacious only in a partial degree. It cleanseth from *all* sin: but this in its completeness, will not be experienced until the Christian comes to the gates of the Holy City, into which nothing that defileth can enter.

Our new guides, dissenting from these views,

insist that the Gospel proposes, not merely an absolute cure of our spiritual maladies, but an immediate absolute cure. "If the disease is total, the remedy to be adequate must cure totally. The Gospel-plan does this. It is not a palliative but an eradicator. In some bodily diseases, there remains, after healing, a tendency to a relapse. But is this the kind of cure made by the Great Healer of soul-diseases? Is not His power sufficient to make a more radical cure, even to the removing all tendency to sin? We assert without fear of successful contradiction that Christ, through our faith, makes as radical a cure of the sin-leprosy of the soul, as He made in the case of the physical leper that once stood in His incarnate presence. This man was not left with any proclivity to that terrible disease: and in like manner, the believer is not only freed from all sin, but from all *tendency* to sin,—albeit, there is in his case, as in Adam's, a possibility of his becoming sinful."* This, we are told, is far more honorable to God than the common view. "Can it be that our Heavenly Father desires less than the perfect sanctification of His children? Is He not more glorified by their deliverance from all sin, than by their being left to struggle with inbred sin

* Anonymous.

through life?" However plausible this may be, it is very fallacious.

The question is not as to God's power, but as to the mode and measure in which He may be pleased to put forth His power. Nor are we in any position to argue, except from His own declarations and from the event, as to what may be most for His glory. The moment you discard this principle, you are at sea without chart or compass. When you ask, "Would not the instant sanctification of His children redound more to His honor, than a gradual growth in grace?" it is easy to ask in reply, Would it not reflect the highest glory on His perfections, to bring all men everywhere to immediate repentance? to make every sinner complete in holiness, at his regeneration? to purify His Church from all its formalism, lukewarmness, avarice, pride, discord, unbelief, and other deformities? Would it not seem to have been most for His glory, to save the race four thousand years of darkness and death, by causing the atoning sacrifice to be offered the day Adam and Eve were driven out of Eden? or, to have kept up an unbroken series of Pentecostal revivals, which should have carried the Gospel to the ends of the earth in a single century? or, should He now unveil the

Messiah to all the seed of Abraham, pour out his Spirit upon all flesh, and fill all human hearts with His grace and truth? Questions like these come unbidden to the lips. They reach into a sphere which our puny faculties cannot penetrate. One thing is clear: God has never governed the world as we would have governed it. His power is infinite, and He hates sin. But it has not seemed good to Him to endow His children with perfect holiness here. Some of the probable reasons and substantial advantages of this arrangement, are apparent. Not to go into so broad a field, we are reminded that, instead of conducting the emancipated Hebrews directly to Canaan, as He might have done, He sent them to wander up and down in the desert,—not without a motive. "Thou shalt remember all the way which the Lord thy God led thee these forty years in the wilderness, to humble thee, and to prove thee, to know what was in thine heart, whether thou wouldest keep His commandments or no." (Deut. 8 : 2.) It has been the common feeling of evangelical Christians, that their own experience of the "wilderness-life," in revealing them to themselves, unveiling the perils of the way, humbling their pride, teaching them their own frailty and corruption, and disclosing the might and majesty, the faithfulness and sympathy, of their Lord, and the unsearchable riches of His grace, surrounds the Divine name with a brighter lustre and secures to them a better preparation for heaven, than if they had passed at once from a condition of unmitigated depravity to a state of spotless holiness. Such, in any event, is the economy He has established, and it *must* be for the best. Not to dwell upon the bold assumption, that there are believers from whose hearts "all *tendency* to sin is eradicated" in the present life, we pass on to notice a remarkable development of the prevailing *animus* of this school.

Reference has been made to the intense antipathy they manifest toward the seventh chapter of Romans. The three chapters, of which this is the intermediate one, they regard as their main fortress. No Scriptures are oftener quoted: none more unscrupulously put upon the rack. It might have been supposed that a group of Christian writers, especially writers who profess to be in such intimate communion with God, would exhibit some modesty in proposing a novel interpretation of a portion of Scripture which has engaged the most devout and careful study of hundreds of learned and pious commentators. No one would question their right to interpret it for themselves, and to commend their exposition to others. But to expound such a passage in a way not only unknown to men like Henry, Scott, Poole, Doddridge, Chalmers,* Hodge, and their compeers, but in flat contradiction of their views; to do this, entirely upon their own responsibility, without citing a single Biblical scholar who agrees with them; and to do it in a tone of confidence which actual inspiration could not have made more emphatic; this, to say the least, is not very assuring as to the verity of the exposition they propose. "The *meek* will He guide in judgment; and the meek will He teach His way."

In the scheme we are examining, the seventh chapter of Romans marks, not an habitual experience, but a distinct stage in the religious life of St. Paul, at which, having paused for a while, he goes on to the next stage, chapter eight, where he settles down as his permanent home. With a simplicity which might be pardonable in a stranger to the Christian faith, it is asked, "How can we make these two experiences consistent with each other? It is not possible that they should be the

---

* Chalmers is quoted in the Tract on Romans vii. and elsewhere: but in his Lectures on that chapter he controverts the H. L. views as vehemently as if their publications had been before him at the time. His name will recur hereafter.

coincident condition of a Christian's life; for they are in radical contrast to one another. They must refer to different periods in the experience of Paul, and the important question is, 'Which is the one in which we ought to expect to live?'"* Here is a phenomenon: A believer who has been following Christ, and in most intimate fellowship with him for fifteen, twenty, perhaps thirty years, and has yet to learn that the Christian life is essentially a life of contraries! As well say that the conditions "cannot be coincident," which the same apostle describes in terms like these:— "When I am weak, then am I strong:" "As unknown, and yet well known; as dying, and behold we live; as chastened and not killed; as poor, yet making many rich; as having nothing, and yet possessing all things." It is respectfully submitted, that no conception of the life of God in the soul can even approximate to the truth, which fails to recognize the co-existence of these seeming opposites. The problem, however, is too abstruse for our Higher Life friends. It would be wearisome to cite the passages in which they express their sympathy for the mass of believers, who are leading the "wilderness-life of the seventh chapter," and know nothing of the liberty

* *Tract on Romans VII.*, R. P. S.

and blessedness of those who, like themselves, "have learned the secret of practical holiness." and are "no longer servants but children in their Father's house." "These two states and stages of experience, as they affect the Christian in his own heart and life," are contrasted as "giving to his course the cast of sadness and sighing in the one case, and of exultant joys in the glorious liberty of conscious deliverance, in the other,"* —with much more to the same purpose. That the apostle's experience in Romans seventh should be an enigma to the mind of a rationalist; and that some good men should take it as the experience of an imaginary unconverted sinner, personated by St. Paul for the time; need excite no surprise. But that any earnest Christian who concedes it to be a record of the apostle's own inner life, should protest against it as indicating *a very low stage of piety*, derogatory alike to God and man, is a marvel never observed, it is believed, outside the ranks of this wholly sanctified community. How far they have gone in denouncing it, may be seen by referring to the tract just mentioned, wherein "the experience of the seventh of Romans" is explicitly branded as "GOD-DISHONORING and

* *Higher Christian Life.*

bitterly humiliating,"—an epithet exchanged in "*Walking in the Light*" (p. 98) for "CHRIST-DISHONORING." Such is the audacious language employed to describe a feature of the acknowledged religious life of an inspired apostle, by one professing to have reached that proud elevation towards which, as they inform us, Paul was now struggling! Not only so, but the writer must have known (for their books constantly assert and deplore it) that he was stigmatizing herein, not merely Paul's experience, but that of countless thousands of humble belivers who have lived, as he did, as well in the seventh as in the eighth of Romans. Augustine, Luther, Bradford, Bunyan, Baxter, Edwards, Chalmers, Alexander, McCheyne, and hosts of others of whom the world was not worthy, are implicated in this indictment of a "*God-dishonoring experience.*" And this charge is from the pen of one who evidently brings it forward without the least suspicion that it savors of irreverence, spiritual pride, or uncharitableness. Is *this* what is meant by "living without conscious sin"? And if so, is "consciousness" that trustworthy guide which these teachers assume it to be?

To look a little more closely into this exegetical theory,—If it be claimed that Paul is here defining, not constituent elements of the Christian life, but distinct stages which we pass as we do successive railway stations, then they must relinquish both the fifth and sixth chapters or make an admission very humbling to the apostle, and very damaging to their doctrine. For in the seventh he is in bondage, painfully fighting for deliverance. At v. 25 he emerges suddenly from his conflict; experiences his "second conversion;" and enters upon the joy of an unsinning obedience, which thenceforth becomes his normal condition. Now, turning to the opening of the fifth chapter, we read: "Therefore being justified by faith, we have peace with God through our Lord Jesus Christ: by whom also we have access by faith into this grace wherein we stand and rejoice in hope of the glory of God." Surely when he wrote this, he was "in the Higher Life." That he was there when he penned the sixth chapter, is so plain to the minds of these writers that they marvel that any one should doubt it. But in the seventh chapter, he falls from his high estate, plunges into a sea of darkness and turmoil, and allows his inward corruptions to wrestle with him in a way utterly discreditable to a Christian man. Presently, however (v. 25), a strong arm rescues him, and bears him up again into the beatific realm of the Higher Life, and there he stays—at least until he has written the eighth chapter. It appears, then, that in penning the fifth and sixth chapters, St. Paul was in the enjoyment and exercise of "practical holiness." This priceless blessing he somehow lost. Thereupon he wrote the seventh chapter, to describe and bewail his sad condition. From this he after a while obtained deliverance; and then wrote the eighth. That he spent the residue of his life "in the eighth chapter," is sheer assumption. His Epistles to the Galatians and the Philippians, interpreted by their rules, furnish proof that he once and again fell back "into the seventh chapter." And so the portrait of this thrice-honored servant of God, which we are invited to contemplate, is that of a man whose piety is alternately flickering and flaming, and who is kept through life oscillating between holiness and sin, between slavery and freedom, between ecstasy and misery. All this sounds like travesty; but it is a just and accurate summary of the exposition demanded by the Higher Life canons of interpretation. And it shows, if anything could, how artificial and capricious are the methods of explaining Scripture enforced by the exigencies of that system. Whereas if we take with us the simple principle, that the apostle is here dealing with the spiritual life, not merely in its gradations, but also in its *radical and permanent elements*, these four pregnant chapters at once become a luminous and consistent whole, replete with mingled instruction, admonition, and comfort.

The expressions which ensnare our new expositors are *inter alia* those which represent believers as "dead to sin;" "freed from sin;" "crucified with Christ;" "risen with Christ;" and the like. If phrases of this sort are to be accepted without qualification, they import that the persons to whom they pertain are absolutely sinless: for the dead cannot sin: the crucified cannot sin: those who are as much "alive unto God" as Jesus was after His resurrection, cannot sin. This is the Perfectionism of Oberlin, and it has the advantage of taking the expressions according to the letter. But the Higher Life school reject this teaching, although inconsistently complaining that "ordinary Christians" tone down the apostle's meaning. What less are they themselves doing when they explain these terms as referring to conscious sin, and practical holiness; a holiness, a love, and an obedience, that are indeed perfect, according to the full measure of the light one may now have, but not necessarily perfect as indicating an actual eradication of all the hidden roots of sin. Now to Perfectionists of this type we are warranted in saying, If you may thus restrict the apostle's meaning, why may not we restrict it? What right have you to say to us, "You must not take St. Paul at precisely what he says, for that would be the figment of an immaculate holiness; but you must interpret him as setting forth that mitigated type of perfect sanctification which *we* believe in"? Our answer is, We shall do neither. In common with the great body of evangelical expositors, theologians, and private Christians, we hold that the true believer is "dead to sin," inasmuch as he is released from its *dominion*, both forensically and personally. It was nailed to the cross: when Christ died, the believer died: and there is now no condemnation to him. In his regeneration the sceptre of sin was broken, and he was emancipated from its thraldom: but it still harasses and vexes whom it cannot destroy. Sin has received its death-wound; but it has vitality enough to struggle on—the old man against the new—as long as life lasts.

We have already seen that in saying to the Colossians, "Ye are dead," (*ye died,*) the apostle *could* not intend that they had reached an unsinning condition. The same thing is equally apparent here in the sixth of Romans, and for a similar reason. For one of the favorite proof-verses of these writers, which they quote on all occasions, is instantly followed by an exhortation which *implies* that the usual explanation, as distinguished from theirs, is the true one: "Likewise reckon ye also yourselves to be dead indeed unto sin, but alive unto God through Jesus Christ our Lord." (v. 11.) This means, we are told, that the believer is, and must so "reckon" or adjudge himself to be, discharged of his inward warfare, and so imbued with the life of Christ that he has ceased from sin. So pronounced are they in insisting upon this interpretation, that it may be useful to ask whether they themselves are prepared to stand by it. It is the Christians of Rome, as a body, to whom St. Paul says, "Reckon yourselves to be dead to sin:" that is, *Believe* that you are now cleansed from all sin and living a sinless life. Of course, he could not tell them to believe what was not true. Therefore, if this view of the passage be correct, the Roman Church *was made up of persons who were perfectly sanctified*, and who were bound so to regard themselves. By no craft of logic can this conclusion be evaded. Do the Higher Life writers believe it? Do they believe that here was an entire Christian community, all of whom had entered upon "the way of practical holiness," and were living "without conscious sin"? A rarer phenomenon this, than any ecclesiastical annalist has discovered among the records of eighteen centuries. And one, it may be added, which is clearly proved to have only an imaginary existence by the contents of the Epistle itself. The animadversions of the apostle upon various errors and faults more or less prevalent in the Church at Rome, show plainly enough that *he* did not look upon it as a Church "without spot or wrinkle." Nor is it to be supposed for a moment, that any teacher or convert of the new doctrine, so regards it. What then becomes of the use to which this text is perverted? If the apostle did not mean, by this language, to tell the Roman Christians that they must "reckon themselves to be in an unsinning condition," how can it be pretended that the Christians of *Philadelphia* or of *London* are here instructed by him to believe that *they* have reached an unsinning condition? Does the verse mean more for them, than it did for those to whom Paul inscribed it?—What he does say is obvious enough to one who holds that Scripture is to be interpreted by Scripture, and who will note the tenor of the apostle's inference, as follows: "Let not sin, therefore, *reign* in your mortal body, that ye should obey it in the lusts thereof. Neither yield ye your members as instruments of unrighteousness unto sin; but yield yourselves unto God as those that are alive from the dead, and your members as instruments of righteousness unto God: for sin shall not have *dominion* over you." This were strange counsel to give to a band of pilgrims who were already careering in triumph along a pathway of sinless obedience; while it is most apposite to a caravan who are contesting every step of the way with the adversaries still lurking in their breasts. Dr. Chalmers shall speak for us here:

"'Let not sin,' says the apostle, 'reign in your mortal body, that ye should obey it in the lusts thereof.' Here we cannot fail to perceive how widely diverse the injunction of the apostle would have been if instead of saying, 'Let not sin *reign* in your mortal bodies,' he had said, 'Let sin be rooted out of your mortal bodies;' or if instead of saying, Obey not its lusts, he had bid us eradicate them. It were surely a far more enviable state to have no inclination to evil at all, than to be oppressed with the constant forthputting of such an inclination, and barely to keep it in check under the power of some opposing principle. Could we attain the higher state on this side of time, we would become on earth what angels are in heaven, whose every desire runs in the pure current of love and loyalty to a God of holiness. But if doomed to the lower state, during all the days of our abode in the world, then are we given to understand that the life of a Christian is a life of vigilant and unremitting warfare; that it consists in the struggle of two adverse elements, and the habitual prevalence of one of them; that in us and closely around us, there is a besetting enemy who will not quit his hold of us, till death paralyze his grasp and so let us go; and that from this sore conflict of the Spirit lusting against the flesh, and the flesh against the Spirit, we shall not be conclusively delivered, till our present tainted materialism shall be utterly taken down; and that the emancipated soul shall not have free and unconfined scope for its heavenly affections, until it has burst its way from the prison-hold of its earthly tabernacle." *

To this may be added the testimony of one of the great lights of the Church of England—one whose eminent piety, and profound insight into the intricacies of experimental religion, entitle him to be heard with the utmost respect. In his

* Lectures on Romans vi.

elaborate and searching discourse upon Romans 8 : 13, on the "Great Duty of Mortification," Bishop Hopkins says: "There are a sort of enthusiasts risen up among us who, by pretending to that, in this life, unattainable privilege of a perfect immunity from all sin, do make mortification inconsistent with mortality; and while they promise to themselves that liberty which God never promised them, they are become the servants of corruption. St. John frequently gives these men the plain lie: 'If we say that we have no sin, we deceive ourselves and the truth is not in us. If we say that we have not sinned, we make God a liar, and the truth is not in us.' (1st Ep. 1 : 8, 10.) This is that which the manifold falls, the grievous outcries, the bitter repentings, the broken bones, and the bloodied consciences even of the best and perfectest saints on earth, have too sadly attested beyond all contradiction,—unless it be from those men to whom customariness hath made the difference between sinning and forbearing to sin unperceivable. It is indeed the sincere desire and endeavor of every child of God, so thoroughly to mortify corruption, that it should never more stir nor tempt; never more move, nor break forth, unto eternity. Oh, it would be a blessed word of promise if God should say to us concerning our lusts, as Moses did to the Israelites, 'Those Egyptians whom you have seen this day pursuing your souls, ye shall see them again no more for ever.' But no: these Canaanites are suffered to be thorns in our eyes and scourges in our sides, to sweeten the place of our future rest. When we are most victorious over them, all we can do is to make them subject and tributary: for they have so possessed the fastnesses of our souls, that there is but one mortification can drive them out, and that is our dissolution. It was only sin that brought death into the world; and it is only death that can carry sin out of the world. So that every true Christian is another Samson: he slays more of the uncircumcised at his death, than he did in all his lifetime before." In all this, however, there is no ground for discouragement. These corruptions cannot be extirpated, but you may wage a successful war against them: for the Spirit of God is your ever-present Helper. He it is who begins, carries forward, and consummates the entire work of sanctification. "What are the deeds of the body to the power of the Spirit of Holiness? Wilt thou shrink from this engagement, when thou hast so much the odds of thy corruptions? when the Spirit of God stands by to encourage thee, to help and assist thee? Never yet was it known that a soul who engaged the Spirit of God in the quarrel, came off with less than a victory."

Bishop Hopkins, having in view a type of Perfectionism which had run into Antinomianism, made use of certain expressions which it were unjust to apply to the Higher Life preachers, who, it is believed, are eminently conscientious and devout Christians. But that the doctrine of present Perfection, under any and all its forms, includes a latent, insidious, and potent tendency to Antinomianism, is attested through the whole course of ecclesiastical history. It is one of those arts in which the teacher is very apt to be outstripped by his pupils, who, ordinarily, as in the case under review, go from bad to worse. This, however, by the way.—The two distinguished writers just quoted, find, in the Epistle to the Romans, no hint of a perfect holiness attainable in the present life; but abundant tokens of a conflict with indwelling sin which every believer must wage until he puts off his mortality. These extracts illustrate the nature of the contest so affectingly described by the apostle in his obnoxious seventh chapter: "That which I do, I allow not; for what I would, that do I not; but what I hate, that do I. . . . For I know that in me, that is, in my flesh, dwelleth no good thing: for to will is present with me, but how to perform that which is good, I find not. For the good that I would, I do not; but the evil which I would not, that I do." (See the whole passage.)

Here, it is peremptorily maintained, we have a revolting exhibit of St. Paul's inner life; the degrading experience of a man who was manacled and fettered; a stranger as yet to that "practical holiness" which he was soon to achieve through the merciful intervention of the Lord Jesus Christ. It may be of small moment to these writers, that they stand so much alone in their estimate of this vivid picture. Men who claim to have been commissioned to roll off from the Church the stigma of keeping the doctrine of sanctification by faith almost out of sight "for eighteen centuries," can afford to contemn the suggestions even of illustrious scholars and divines whose studies in the sacred oracles have won for them, by general consent, the title of Masters in Israel. Dr. Chalmers shall again speak, alike for the august brotherhood of evangelical expositors and for the mass of "ordinary Christians." He does not think the apostle quite so abject a Christian as his critics will have him to be, in the chapter under review:

"The confessions which are recorded here (Rom. 7 : 16, 17) are not those of a degraded criminal, but those of a struggling and heavenly-minded Christian, who was now forcing his way among the sins and the sanctities of the inner man, and far above the level of our ordinary world, was soaring amid the spiritual alternations of cloud and of sunshine up to the heights of angelic sacredness. . . . It argues a very exalted Christianity, when the glory of God is the habitual and paramount impulse that gives movement to the footsteps of our history in the world. But, think you, that when a man's heart comes to be visited by this ambition, that then it is he makes his escape from the complaint of doing what he would not? It only thickens the contest, and multiplies the chances of mortification, and furnishes new topics of humility to the disciple,— and in the very proportion too that he urges and ascends and strikes loftier aims along the course of his progressive holiness. And so it follows, that he who is highest in acquirement, is sure to be deepest in lowly and contrite tenderness: for just as the desires of his spirit mount higher, will the damp and the deadness and the obstructions of the flesh be more felt as a grief and an encumbrance to him. So that while in the body this soliloquy of the apostle will be all his own; and so far from conceiving of it as the appropriate utterance for a natural and unconverted man, it is just as we are the more saintly, that we shall feel our readiness to coalesce with it as the fittest vehicle of hearts smitten with the love of purest excellence, yet burdened under a sense of distance and deficiency therefrom. . . . Here the accursed nature is still present and galling with its offensive solicitations, the regenerated spirit; so that when weighed down by indolence, or frozen into apathy, or betrayed into uncharitable thoughts and uncharitable wishes, or led to seek the desires of its own selfishness more than God's honor, to rejoice in its exemption from punishment more than to aspire after its exemption from sin, to be more vehement for the object of being safe than for the object of being sanctified,—the consciousness of these, which give no disturbance either to the unChristian man or to the Christian in his infancy, is still in reserve to humble and keep down even the most accomplished believer; to assure him still of the many things that he does which he would not; to keep him at the post of dependence where he may join with the apostle in mourning over his own wretchedness, and with the Psalmist in exclaiming, 'Who can understand his errors? Cleanse thou me from secret faults. Search me, O God, and know my heart; try me and know my thoughts; and see if there be any wicked way in me, and lead me in the way everlasting.'"

If it were needful to sustain Chalmers's view of the conflict which the apostle waged with himself, and which is waged by all Christians, Perfectionists excepted, Romaine's three Treatises on the "Life," the "Walk," and the "Triumph," "of Faith," are, as it were, saturated with it. And many pages might be filled with lists of authorities in full accord with these excellent men on this most weighty subject. With what amazement would any of them have listened to an experience involving, by fair implication, some such transmutation of the seventh of Romans as the following!—

"I know that the law is spiritual, and I too am spiritual. That which I do, I allow: for what I would not, that do I not; but what I love, that do I. To will is present with me, and I find how to perform that which is good. For the good that I would, I always do; and the evil which I would not, I never do. I find in myself a law that when I would do good, good is present with me. For not only do I delight in the law of God after the inward man; but I see no law in my members which wars against the law of my mind. It was once otherwise with me: the flesh used to lust against the Spirit, but that has ceased: infinite grace rescued me. And while I still have outward foes, I now have none within. One law controls my whole inner being. The merit all belongs to Christ: but I have the blessed consciousness of never offending Him. My will is absorbed in His will: and I not only *will* to serve Him without sin day by day, month by month, yea, year by year; but I actually do it."

I am not able to see that there is here any misconception of what the Higher Life School challenge to themselves as their personal experience; for it is the simple *reverse* of that "God-dishonoring experience" of the apostle, which they so habitually hold up to reprobation. Whether of the two savors most of a genuine experience, it must be left to each person to decide for himself. It will be no strange thing if most unsophisticated Christians, in passing upon St. Paul's record, should side rather with Chalmers and Hopkins and Romaine, than with those whose cherished distinction it is to have got beyond all such conflicts with deep-seated depravity, as that which he delineates and deplores.

CHAPTER VIII.

"HALF-TRUTHS"—COMMANDS AND PROMISES—PRAYER.

LET it not be inferred that, by reason of this war between the flesh and the Spirit, the ordinary Christian life is essentially a life of gloom and despondency. Such is the impression conveyed by the current phraseology of the Perfectionist writers. We do, indeed, maintain that the discordant element which the New Testament styles "the flesh," cleaves to the believer through life. But it is the ordained law of the economy of redemption, that this principle shall gradually weaken and the adverse principle of grace wax stronger and stronger. There are, in the experience of most Christians, occasional seasons of sore temptation or trial, when the inward strife rages with a violence which seems to menace the soul's moorings. But for these assaults they have an unfailing resource. The Master they love, succors and relieves them: and then they may be heard triumphantly exclaiming, "Thanks be to God which giveth us the victory through our Lord Jesus Christ." In the settled course of things, the believer is daily reminded that he carries about with him some remains of his native depravity. And the consciousness not only makes him the more watchful, humble, and prayerful; but enhances his gratitude for the abounding mercy which has dissolved the sway of these baleful tendencies, and opened to his faith the inexhaustible stores of grace and comfort treasured up in his Divine Head. All his desires, aims, and efforts, are enlisted on the gracious side of his nature. His aspirations are God-ward. He longs after holiness, and cannot be satisfied unless he is sensibly imbibing more and more of the mind which is in Christ. The yoke he wears is an easy yoke; and the service he renders is a cheerful service—one that points unerringly to a future and complete deliverance from all sin and all sorrow. But the more absolute his assurance of this high destiny, the more vividly alive is he to the foul dregs of corruption which still tenant the recesses of his bosom. It is the universal sentiment of Christian casuists, outside the various Perfectionist circles, that the holier a believer becomes, the quicker is he to discern, to lament, and to confess, the faults and errors which still deface his character and impair the plenary integrity of his obedience. The stronger the celestial light thrown in upon his soul, the more distinctly are its blemishes revealed: the more pure and fervent his love to Christ, the keener his regret that it falls so immeasurably short of what it should be.

As bearing alike upon what has been said of the misuse of 1 Cor. 1 : 30 and Col. 3 : 3, and upon what is to follow, it will be pertinent to quote here the opening paragraph of one of the Higher Life tracts, entitled "*Half Truths:*"

"Few devices of the enemy of souls are more successful than that of inducing Christians to stop at half truths. Failing in his efforts to hinder their grasping part of a truth, he prevents them from going on to apprehend it in all its perfection and symmetry, and so presents to the world a mutilated representation of God's work in the salvation of men. We can scarcely name any errorists who have not held and pressed some portions of God's Truth, which have been overlooked or little taught by others. Their strength is in the portion of truth which they earnestly advocate, and their failure lies in the neglect of other related truths. One side of an arch may be of enduring granite, but if the other be of crumbling sandstone, the bridge has only as much strength as is in the weaker side. In the consciousness of our proneness to limited, one-sided views of the Gospel, our narrow capacities, our blighted faculties, and at the best our yet imperfect apprehension, well may we cry, hour by hour, from the depths of our hearts, 'Open Thou mine eyes, that I may behold wondrous things out of Thy law!'"

These excellent remarks (by "R. P. S.") could not be more aptly illustrated than they are by the author himself and his associates in their habitual method of dealing with the Scriptures. They fitly open the way for a complaint against the Higher Life teachers for their treatment, in connection with the closing verses of Romans vii., of "ordinary Christians." Over and over do they state it as the common practice of such Christians, to pause at the apostle's pathetic cry for succor, without appropriating the exultant pæan of victory which follows. To quote a single paragraph: "Not that these persons are not Christians. They have learned that their sins are forgiven through faith in the atonement of Jesus. But they have not yet learned that Jesus, through faith in His name, is the Deliverer from the power of sin as well as from its penalty. So they cry out, 'Who shall deliver me from the body of this death?' And *there they stop. There their experience stops.* So far they have come, but no farther. While they of the second class [themselves] ask the question indeed, 'Who shall deliver me from the body of this death?' but answer it in the same breath by finishing the quotation in the apostle's exultant words, 'I thank God, through Jesus Christ our Lord.'" *—One is ready to ask, on reading this extraordinary statement, whether it be one of the prerogatives of those who have obtained "the blessing," to talk at random about less-favored Christians. Not even an unsinning disciple should venture upon a representation like this, in the way of mere assertion. Let him prove what he has said. Let him bring forward his witnesses to show that "ordinary Christians" do not take Christ as their "Deliverer from the power of sin," and that they know nothing of the joy of that sweet psalm of praise, "I thank God, through Jesus Christ our Lord." Until these affirmations are proved, he lies open to the imputation of presenting a portraiture of his fellow-Christians which is not warranted by any facts within the reach of common observers.

It is not pleasant to be obliged to add a second

* W. E. Boardman.

instance in which these writers display a similar lack of ingenuousness, in dealing with this same passage. Their theory requires that the apostle, having thrown off at v. 25 all the "beggarly elements" of his inchoate sanctification, and risen to the proud elevation of "practical holiness," should enter at once into the glorious liberty of the eighth chapter, the fruit and evidence of his moral perfection. That he actually does this, is one of the common-places of their books. You meet with it in all their publications, large and small. They never weary in pointing out, that St. Paul left the totality of his body of sin and death in the dismal seventh chapter, and, in its last verse, spread his wings for a flight into the refulgent realm of spotless holiness. Now what must be thought of the candor of these teachers, when it is mentioned, that the apostle not only does not say this, but says *what is not compatible with it?* They have the assurance to upbraid other Christians, with "clipping the seventh of Romans at both ends, to make it suit their experience."* Would it be believed that they themselves never quote the closing sentence of this chapter? "We must not content ourselves (so we are often admonished) with half-texts." Phy-

* W. E. B.

sician, heal thyself. There are probably scores of instances in which they bisect the last verse of chapter seventh, in the most unscrupulous way, not only without the least hint that they are not giving the whole verse, but actually asserting (see W. E. B. above) that they *do* "finish the quotation." No charity can blind one's eyes to the reason. The close of the verse is no less fatal to their whole scheme of interpretation, than it is pertinent to the apostle's delineation of his own inner life. The whole verse runs thus: "I thank God, through Jesus Christ our Lord. So then with the mind I myself serve the law of God; but with the flesh the law of sin." In the solitary instance (solitary, it is confidently believed) in which this last clause is cited, an attempt is made to turn its edge: "So then with the mind I myself serve the law of God; but with the flesh, (*when he was in it*) the law of sin."* This will not do. The parenthetical limitation is demanded by the Higher Life theory, but if the author consulted his Greek Testament, he must have seen that the sentence contains but one verb, and that verb is in the present tense. The verb is not even repeated: "*I serve* the law of God and the law of sin." It is intensely arbi-

* *Tract on Romans VII.*, by R. P. S.

trary to take the verb in the present tense in the first clause, and in the past tense in the second. He does *not* say, "When I was in the flesh, I *served* the law of sin." He does say, "With the flesh I *serve* the law of sin." As if he had said: "I thank God that through the Lord Jesus Christ, I obtain deliverance from those corrupt lusts which war against my soul. But while assured of this and rejoicing in it; while it is my only aim and my only happiness to serve the law of God with all my heart, and with the pledge of ultimate and glorious triumph; it humbles me to feel that that hateful law of sin of which I have been speaking, though its power is broken, keeps its place in my heart, and still exacts from me a reluctant and humiliating service." This interpretation is demanded alike by the syntax of the passage and by the general drift of the whole argument. And it is of ill omen that the verse should be tortured to say what it does not say, lest it may subvert a favorite speculation. Let it suffice to add that there is no incongruity whatever between the true view of the sentence and the opening of the eighth chapter, wherein the apostle recurs to the forensic statement of the believer's deliverance from *condemnation;* and then goes on to expatiate in glowing terms, upon his being both justified and sanctified, and upon the exalted privileges and hopes which constitute the immortal dowry of all who are in Christ.

We have already had occasion to see that certain texts relied upon to establish the doctrine of "practical holiness," cannot legitimately be put to that use. It is a very curious assumption of this school, that the Divine commands, exhortations, and promises, are to be taken as involving immediate and plenary results:—*e. g.*, "Who gave Himself for us that He might redeem us from *all* iniquity." "The very God of peace sanctify you *wholly*." "Who hath chosen us in Him that we should be holy, and without blame before Him in love." "He that dwelleth in love, dwelleth in God, and God in him." "But, speaking the truth in love, may grow up into Him in all things, which is the Head." "Whether, therefore, ye eat or drink, or whatsoever ye do, do all to the glory of God." "From all your filthiness and from all your idols will I cleanse you. . . . And I will put my Spirit within you, and cause you to walk in my statutes, and ye shall keep my judgments and do them." "I will put my laws into their mind, and write them in their hearts." Certainly God here promises that all His children shall be graced with perfect holiness. It were puerile to argue that therefore all men—for it is obligatory upon all—are holy. Test this principle by the text: "Be ye therefore perfect, even as your Father which is in heaven is perfect." (Matt. 5 : 48.) Here is an explicit command. Does the command prove that it has been complied with? Our Higher Life friends, as already observed on this verse, dare not claim this even for themselves: for the "perfection" here enjoined is the absolute perfection of God the Father—to which they make no pretension. That the Gospel makes provision for the complete sanctification of all believers, and that God has promised this great blessing, is true. But where are we taught that it is to be theirs in the present life? In similar terms, He has promised them deliverance from toilsome labor, from sickness and pain and sorrow. If the former class of promises must be interpreted of this life, why not the latter? Both will be fulfilled, but not here and now. The incipiency is here. He does put His Spirit in the hearts of His people. He lays upon them the loving constraint of an habitual striving after entire holiness. He guides and assists them in all their work and warfare; and thus disciplines them for their final investiture with robes of spotless purity. Should not this suffice?

In the same inconclusive manner do these

writers argue from the promises concerning prayer. Not to cite the numerous passages which refer to this subject, their chief reliance is upon 1 John 5 : 14, 15 : "And this is the confidence that we have in Him, that if we ask anything according to His will, He heareth us: and if we know that He hear us whatsoever we ask, we know that we have the petitions that we desired of Him." Here, we are told, is an express promise. That you should become perfect in holiness, must be "according to His will." Pray, then, for perfect holiness, and you are warranted to believe that it *is* yours: you "*know* that you *have* the petition you desired of Him."— This is very plausible; but it will not stand. It rests upon the assumption that your perfect and instant sanctification is "according to the will of God." What evidence have you that He "wills" it in any such sense as you put upon the words? Are there not millions of believers praying daily to be effectually delivered from sin, and is the prayer answered otherwise than by a partial and progressive deliverance? Are not these same Christians praying, as the pious of all ages have been, "Thy kingdom come; thy will be done in earth as it is in heaven"? Is not this "according to the will of God"? and has it been answered literally? Did not Paul pray for the entire sanctification of the Ephesians, the Philippians, the Thessalonians, and were his prayers immediately answered, and answered as to all of them?—for of course he prayed for all. Clearly you have no manner of right to assume that your prayer for perfect holiness has been granted at once, and that you *are* thus holy because you have asked to be. Our gracious Father is the Hearer of Prayer. But He loves us too well to allow us to dictate precisely when and how our prayers shall be answered. Answered they will be, if offered in faith: but, peradventure, in ways we had not imagined. As shown by these books, the one thought of a Higher Life disciple in presenting this petition, is, of an instant, direct, and unqualified, translation into a condition of "practical holiness." God may see fit to adopt no such summary method with you. He may answer your prayer for sanctification by showing you unknown depths of deceit and impurity in your heart, allowing Satan to assail you, visiting you with sore trials, disclosing to you the fulness of grace and mercy there is in Christ, and through the effectual working of His Spirit in your breast, nourishing your faith, your humility and self-distrust and patience and hope and love; and by these and other means gradually moulding you into His own image. This may not be your way of attaining personal holiness: it is too tedious and painful. But it is the way in which He has been wont to lead those of His children whom He would adorn with His choicest jewelry: and *they* have not questioned, even while here, that it was the best way. Think you they will question it in heaven?

CHAPTER IX.

PASSIVITY vs. ACTIVITY—FAITH RESTRICTED AND SCRIPTURE SLIGHTED.

THE contrast between the scheme we are examining, and the New Testament, in their relative conceptions of the Christian life, is aptly expressed by the words *Passivity* and *Activity*. The topic has already been noticed, but it is too important to be dismissed without further consideration. The unbiassed reader who peruses any half dozen of the publications of this school, and then takes up the New Testament, will find himself all at once in as different an atmosphere as that of the traveller who goes up out of the still, hazy, enervating air of a secluded Swiss valley, into the fresh, breezy, sparkling ether of the surrounding Alps. They have displayed a marvellous ingenuity in reducing the "whole duty of man" to *a solitary requirement*. When one thinks of the multifarious relations, obligations, temptations, dangers, pleasures, and trials, comprised in the inspired exhibition of the Christian's calling, it would seem beyond a seraph's skill to condense this vast, complex scheme into a single brief formula. But our Higher Life expositors have essayed the resolution of this problem, and, as they fancy, with success.

To guard against misapprehension, let it be repeated just here, that "ordinary Christians" recognize Christ as the source of their spiritual life: that they feel themselves to be nothing, and to be able to do nothing, without Him: that by His Holy Spirit He reveals His truth to them in its various aspects of doctrine, precept, warning, reproof, promise, and comfort, especially the truth concerning His atoning blood; and that thus, invigorating their faith (which feeds upon the word), enlivening their gratitude, quickening their zeal, and giving them renewed energy and ardor in the ceaseless contest with their common foes, He "sanctifies them *through His truth.*" Christ dwells in them that they may abound in the fruits of righteousness, and work the work which He has given them to do.

In the adverse scheme, Christ dwells in His people that they may not work. With a tiresome iteration we are told, Having taken Christ as your sanctification, the thing you have to do, and all you have to do, is, to *continue to exercise faith in Him*, and to *believe* that you *are* abiding in Him. "Dost thou believe that God dwelleth in thee, and thou in Him? For if thou dost, thou *art* abiding in Christ." * As this unscriptural and deluding sentiment recurs very often, suppose we test it by an example. Mother Ann Lee, the Shaker celebrity, confidently "believed" and taught that "Christ dwelt in her." Did He dwell in her? Again: "Believing, resting, abiding,—these are my part: He does all the rest." "If I am dead and God lives in me, what does He do it for? Is it not that He may speak for me, live for me, walk for me—that He may, in short, work in me that which is well pleasing in His sight? Oh, I am persuaded that if Christians only knew the life God would live in them *if they would let Him*, they would never try to live again themselves." In answer to the question, "What is meant by growing in grace?" we are told with characteristic modesty: "It is difficult to answer this question, because so few people have any conception of what the grace of God really is." Then, pressing to an extreme the beautiful illustrations employed by the Saviour, the writer proceeds to argue that

* H. W. S.

because a child and a lily grow without self-effort, so the believer grows. "Many Christians think to accomplish it by toiling and spinning and stretching and straining, and pass their lives in such a round of self-effort as is a weariness to contemplate. . . . You need make no efforts to grow. But let your efforts instead be all concentrated on this, that you abide in the Vine. . . . Give up all your efforts after growing, and simply *let* yourselves grow. Leave it all to the Husbandman whose care it is, and who alone is able to manage it. . . . Abide in the Vine. *Let* the life from Him flow through all your spiritual veins. Interpose no barrier to His mighty life-giving power, working in you all the good pleasure of His will." "He is not asking thee in thy poor weakness, to do it thyself: He only asks thee to yield thyself to Him that He may work in thee to will and to do of His good pleasure. Thy part is to *yield thyself:* His part is to *work:* and never, never will He give thee any command, which is not accompanied by ample power to obey it."* [Can anything exceed the temerity of this writer? Has not Christ, as just now pointed out, commanded *every* disciple (Matt. 5 : 48) to be as perfect as God the Father? and

* *The Christian's Secret.*

have they "received ample power to obey it?"]

Doctor Payson once expressed as follows, his estimate of certain "romantic" sentiments to which he had listened, on growing in grace: "By religious romance I mean the indulgence of unwarranted expectations; expectations *that our sins are to be subdued at once*, in some uncommon way or by some uncommon means—just as a man would expect to become rich by drawing a prize in a lottery, or in some other hap-hazard way. We cannot, indeed, expect too much if we regulate our expectations by the word of God; but we may expect more than He warrants us to expect, and when our unwarranted expectations are disappointed, we are apt to sink into despondency. Christians whose natural feelings are strong, are most liable to run into this error. But I know of no way to make progress in holiness but the steady, humble, persevering practice of meditation, prayer, watchfulness, self-denial, and good works. If we use these means, our progress is certain." Such was Payson's idea of the way to grow in grace, as distinguished from the "romantic" views of the Higher Life School.

In the passages quoted above, and habitually in treating of the subject, they virtually represent the inworking of Christ in the believer's soul, as dependent upon his faith—his "undoubting faith:" for "Jesus *cannot* fully save a doubting soul." We must "interpose no hinderance." We "must *let* Him work in us." "It is our part to believe: His part to work." And when we cease, not believing in Him, but believing implicitly that "He is dwelling in us, He ceases working."—How does this comport with the sentiment that our whole salvation is of God? that Christ must be our all in all, and that everything good in us is from Him? Is not faith a part, a very essential part, of salvation? Can the believer "abide in Christ," except as Christ keeps him there? Does not his hold upon Christ depend absolutely upon Christ's hold of him? (See John 10 : 28, 29.) And could anything be more discouraging, than to be told that our communion with Christ is momentarily suspended upon the exercise of a "consecrating" faith which it is our part (without recognizing it as His gift), to keep alive? Not so:

> "I change—He changes not;
> The Christ can never die;
> His love, not mine, the resting-place;
> His truth, not mine, the tie."

These extracts show, again, that the faith so much insisted upon by this school, contemplates purely the *Person* of the indwelling Christ, not the Divine Redeemer,—our Prophet, Priest, and King, as revealed to our faith in His word and by His Spirit. It is the mystical notion of Jesus inhabiting the body and soul of the Christian, and by the immediate and, as it were, physical exercise of His power, "living his life" for him. The believer's sole function consists in "letting" the Son of God do this. It is not that he grows by patient, trusting, adoring *meditation* upon Christ and the great themes of Redemption. This is a Scriptural means of sanctification—very precious, and unhappily too much slighted in this stirring age. It is rather—if one can sift out the meaning of their ambiguous phraseology—a sort of tactual process in which the believer's functions of doing, laboring, contending, achieving, are, not intermediately, not spiritually, but by direct, corporeal contact, prompted, energized, and controlled, by the personal Christ within. That something akin to this is intended, seems to be intimated, as in other expressions, so also by the familiar and daring statement, that "the act of perfect abandonment to Christ in all His offices of mercy, cleansing, power, and guidance, places the soul in Christ's hands, and *makes Him alone responsible*, if we may so speak, for all results.

Our responsibility *ends with the abiding*; for then He Himself works in us both to will and to do of His good pleasure." *—And pray, how long would our "abiding" last, if it depended upon ourselves? And where has He told us to hold Him "responsible" for our obedience? And how oddly would it have sounded had the apostle said: "To me to live is Christ, and therefore the whole responsibility for my doing what I ought, attaches to Him"! Have any of us so learned Christ?

We shall be met, no doubt, with the question: "Do we not constantly affirm that it is God who worketh in us to will and to do of His good pleasure?" An unfortunate question. There is no Scripture more frequently quoted by them. It occurs over and over in single tracts; and some of their larger volumes fairly bristle with it. But, like the closing verse of the seventh of Romans, it supplies a notable example of their facility in using "half-truths," or cutting texts in two. Would it be believed, they always quote one-half of this verse, clearly because the dismembered fragment may be made tributary to their system: and the whole verse *never*,—never once, in so far as my researches have gone—for a reason which can neither be denied nor dis-

* *Holiness through Faith.*

guised. The Higher Life theory, as they inculcate it, and as has been shown, has its key in the word, *passivity*. Once "abandoned to Christ," the soul lies in His arms in a state of quiescence—as a musician holds his instrument and plays upon it such melodies as he lists. The half-text in question is even quoted for the purpose of enforcing a lesson the very reverse of that set forth by the apostle. Of the ethics involved in this way of treating an inspired injunction, it must suffice to say, that it does not seem to fit in well with a profession of entire sanctity. " Is not the promise worthy of confidence, that God will work in us to will and to do of His good pleasure, and if He does this, *shall we not have to cease working ourselves?*" And elsewhere: " God worketh in you to will and to do; therefore *cease working.*" Now let us hear the apostle: " *Work out* your own salvation with fear and trembling, for it is God which worketh in you," etc. Reversing the precept of these teachers, and giving a totally different aspect to the sentence, he mentions the inworking of God in their hearts, not as a reason for their "not working," but as a reason for their "working." As if he had said: "You are not to suppose that your salvation is fully accomplished, nor that it is to be consummated by your passively resting in the love of Christ. So far from it, you are to bend all your energies to the working out of your salvation: and *that*, with fear and trembling: for no conscientiousness and solicitude can be deemed excessive, in the pursuit of so momentous an object, exposed as you are on every side to snares and perils. But be of good cheer, and never relax your exertions; for God Himself dwells in you by His Spirit and will work in you as your Guide and Helper." This exhortation, let it be noted, is addressed to St. Paul's favorite Church, at Philippi;—a Church he most warmly commends and for which he has not one word of censure. If it was suited to his beloved Philippians, they must be very advanced Christians to whom it is not suited.—Let us again hear Dr. Chalmers:

"The most complete Scriptural illustration of this doctrine which can be given, is from that celebrated passage where the apostle tells his converts to 'work out their own salvation with fear and trembling, because it is God that worketh in them both to will and to do of His good pleasure.'—A more plain and also more powerful incitement to all diligence, and that throughout every single instant of his course, cannot well be conceived than if the man do not at this instant work to the uttermost of that ability wherewith the Spirit has now invested him, the Spirit will be grieved, and may, on the very next instant, abandon him to his own unsupported feebleness. The relation between the hand that works and the hand by which it is strengthened, furnishes the very strongest, and at the same time most intelligible motive to steady, faithful, and enduring obedience. The man works out his salvation upon the strength of what God has wrought into him; and he does it with fear and trembling, just because most fearfully and tremblingly alive to the thought, that if he does not, God may cease working in him to will any more or to do any more. The doctrine of grace, thus understood, so far from acting as an extinguisher upon human activity, is in truth the very best excitement to it. This dependence between the busy exercise of all your present graces and the supply of new, is the fittest possible tenure on the part of God whereby to hold man to his most constant, most careful, most vigilant obedience. It is felt that the only way of obtaining enlargement and vigor for future services, is to acquit one's self to the uttermost of his present strength, of all his present services; and that thus, and thus alone, he can step by step work his ascending way to a higher and a higher status in practical Christianity. We are aware of the reproach that has been cast on the doctrine of the Spirit's influences; but we trust it will be seen from these views, however imperfectly given, that he who labors in all the present might given, and looks for more, instead of *living in the mystic state of an indolent and expectant quietism,* he of all other men is the most awake to every call of duty—the most painstaking and arduous in every performance of it. There is nothing in that mercy which descends upon us from heaven to supersede the activities of men upon earth. Instead of superseding, its very design is to stimulate these activities. When it works in us, its precise outgoing is just to set us working. Had it operated by an outward or physical constraint upon the hand, then might it only have worked on us to do. But it operates on the inner man, and so as to gain the consent of the heart; and accordingly works in us both to will and to do. We deceive ourselves, then, if we think that under the economy of the Gospel, we are exempted from the assiduities of service; and although we shall never move aright unless breathed upon by an influence from above, yet he only has indeed partaken of that influence who, in practical deference to the authority of God as his Master, holds forth in the history of his life, the aspect of a willing and a doing and a stirring and a painstaking obedience." *

This idea of "working," so eloquently enforced by Dr. Chalmers, is incongruous to a scheme which teaches that the consecrated believer is relegated to a condition of simple quiescence. There is no impression made upon the minds of ordinary readers of the New Testament, more vivid, than that the Christian life is a life of intense activity—a life of watching, of struggle, of combat. To eliminate this element, would involve, not the elision of expressions here and there, but a recasting of the whole phraseology; not a new translation, but a new text. Treatises on sanctification should be distrusted which exclude, and, in deference to their central idea, must exclude, all use of those graphic metaphors employed by the inspired penmen to illustrate the progress of the believer heavenward. "So *run* that ye may obtain. . . . I therefore so *run*, not as uncertainly: so *fight* I, not as one that beateth the air." (1 Cor. 9:24, 26.) "*Striving* according to His working which worketh in me mightily." (Col. 1:29.) "*Fight* the good fight of faith, lay

* Sermon on *The Right Fear and the Right Faith.*

hold on eternal life." "Wherefore seeing we also are compassed about with so great a cloud of witnesses, let us lay aside every weight and the sin which doth so easily beset us, and let us"— what? Let us sit down and allow Christ to run the race for us? Not quite: "Let us run the race that is set before us, looking unto Jesus, the Author and Finisher of our faith." "Brethren, I count not myself to have apprehended: but this one thing I do; forgetting those things which are behind, and reaching forth unto those things which are before, I *press toward the mark* for the prize of the high calling of God in Christ Jesus. Let us, therefore, as many as be perfect, be thus minded." Now, how incompatible with these and similar passages is the theory that, once in Christ, your whole duty consists in keeping up a lively faith in Him, and "letting Him" do all the working and contending. This is not what the apostle says. Ascribing the whole efficiency to his Master, he tells us that it is he himself who runs and strives. "I run." "I fight." "I press toward the mark." "Let *us* run." "So run, that *ye* may obtain." This does not savor much of passivity. Nor can you attempt to compress this style of address into the Higher Life molds without giving the whole thing, grave as it is, a ludicrous aspect. "So let Christ run in you that you may obtain." "Let Christ fight in you the good fight of faith; and let Him lay hold on eternal life." "This one thing I do: I '*let*' the indwelling Christ press toward the mark," etc. Language like this savors both of fatuity and of irreverence: and yet one cannot deny that it is a thoroughly fair mode of testing the theory we are dealing with. The New Testament says, "Work:" the new scheme says, "Stop working." One says, "Strive:" the other, "Lie down." One says, "Run:" the other, "Rest." One says "Fight," the other, "Contend not." "Leave all your watching and wrestling and battling to Jesus: He will do it all." The fascination exerted by this idea—first and last and midst in their creed—"Christ does it all",—is seen very curiously in the sole instance (sole, it is believed) in which they quote the apostle's eloquent and graphic description of the Christian's armor (Eph. 6 : 10–18): "There was my armor waiting for me, but I had never put it on. There was the helmet of salvation; and what is salvation but Christ? There was the breastplate of righteousness; and what is righteousness but Christ? There was the shield of faith; and what is that shield but Christ? And there was the sword of the Spirit;

and what is that sword but the truth of Christ? It is all Christ: and it is all for me." This fanciful explanation, however, designed to do honor to the Saviour, leaves one all in the dark as to the specific nature and use of the several parts of the armor. We all know, and rejoice in knowing, that Christ is so indispensable to us that without His aid we cannot even think a good thought: much less wage a successful war with our subtle and malevolent foes. But when the Christian is set before us in this imposing panoply, we cannot otherwise understand it than as importing that he is a soldier: that his vocation is war: that instead of "resting" and "letting" his great Captain do all the fighting, he himself is to fight. This armor is put upon him, not upon his Leader. And the prominence given to this grand impersonation of the genuine New Testament idea of the Christian life, utterly precludes the conception of a mere passive holiness as being the loftiest type of piety. The higher Christian life of the *Gospel*, is the life which Paul has depicted with such power, and which he himself exemplified—a life, not of immobility and vicarious effort, but of sleepless vigilance, of untiring labor, of incessant conflict, of passionate striving after the glorious prize of the high calling of God, of self-forgetfulness and self-sacrifice in making known to lost sinners the unsearchable riches of Christ. And, blessed be God, there are thousands of disciples, who, like Paul, not counting themselves to have attained, and not discharged from the conflict with indwelling sin, are, in their narrow or, as may be, their broader spheres, following in his steps, leading the same "higher life," and spending and being spent in the service of their Lord. Who cannot name Christians of this type, within the circle of his own observation —Christians who find the joy of the Lord their strength, and who, instead of "rolling all the responsibility of their doing and warring upon Christ," delight in doing their own work under the sweet constraint of His love, and through the grace every hour communicated by His Holy Spirit? And when the skeptic and the scoffer say to us, "Show us what Christianity is, not in your Bibles but in actual life," do we not instinctively point to some humble disciple bearing credentials like these, and reply: "*There* is our religion: does the sun shine upon anything in this world, more beautiful, more attractive, more beneficent?"

It is one of the anomalies of this system, that while ostensibly magnifying faith, it practically *limits and disparages its functions.* "Holiness through Faith," is the chosen watchword of its advocates: the formula which is supposed to discriminate sharply between their doctrine, and the common doctrine of the Church. If there be any denomination of Christians which does not hold that faith is an essential agent in sanctification, it has escaped the notice of the historians. The real difference lies in the respective offices assigned to faith in this important matter. In the Higher Life scheme, the entire stress is laid upon the one act of faith which attends consecration, and is thereafter to be momentarily repeated. You exhaust the requirements of the scheme by continuing, without fail, to look to Christ and "believe that you *do* believe in Him." This assures everything else that may pertain to your proficiency in the life of perfect holiness.

Now of course it is indispensable for the Christian to look to Christ as the sum and source of all light and strength and sanctity. But it is a grave mistake, to suppose that the office of faith begins and ends with this affiance upon the Person of Christ. Sanctification is no such narrow work as this would import. It contemplates the whole character—all the powers, susceptibilities, principles, and passions of the soul. It looks to the mortification of all unholy appetites and habits, and the nutriment and symmetrical unfolding of the understanding, the affections, the moral sense, and the will. It is not possible that a task of such proportions should be accomplished by a specific exercise of faith, however vigorously maintained, which *restricts* its view to the Saviour's Person. "We preach Christ crucified." "I determined not to know anything among you save Jesus Christ and Him crucified." This was the apostle's motto. But he did not interpret it as meaning that he was to do nothing but repeat the story of the crucifixion. His addresses and Epistles show what a variety of subjects were comprehended in his conception of preaching Christ crucified. So it is with faith. The special object of saving faith is the Lord Jesus Christ and whatever pertains to His redeeming work. But as an instrument of sanctification, faith has to do with the whole body of Scripture truth. These writers, as already hinted, are extremely frugal in their references to the *truth* as a vital means of sanctification. Hence their notable reserve as to the Saviour's prayer: "Sanctify them through Thy truth." The valedictory discourse which precedes His prayer, proves that He had respect in this petition, not simply to the truth relating immediately to His atonement, but to the Scriptures at large. Indeed, He Himself explains it when He says, "*Thy word is truth.*" And nothing less can be intended by expressions like these: "Purifying their hearts by faith." Acts 15 : 9. "The obedience of faith." Rom. 1 : 7. "Ye have purified your souls in obeying the truth through the Spirit." 1 Pet. 1 : 22. "The word of God which effectually worketh also in you that believe." 1 Cor. 2 : 13. "Chosen to salvation through sanctification of the Spirit and belief of the truth." 2 Thess. 2 : 13. It would be pleasant to find in formal essays on sanctification like these, the same prominence given to God's truth which it enjoys in the New Testament. In order to its proper efficacy, it must be taken up and assimilated by faith— which is itself, both in its incipiency and growth, the fruit of the Spirit's influence upon the heart. And not one class of truths merely, but all, are made tributary to this end. The Bible is a very large book. Its records spread over many centuries. Its themes are endlessly diversified. It presents truth under countless aspects. But nothing which the infinitely wise God has condescended to write, can be unworthy of our devout study; nothing can be unsuited to our spiritual growth. Faith fails of its mission unless it exercises itself upon the adorable perfections of Jehovah as revealed in His word; upon its commands and promises, its warnings and threatenings, its histories, prophecies, and biographies, its profound doctrines, its exquisite poems, and even its terse apothegms. These are all food for the soul, which, like the body, craves a preponderance, now of this element and now of that: as different constitutions demand different kinds of diet. He who would seek a healthy growth, have all his faculties and affections invigorated, and be ever tending up toward "the stature of a perfect man in Christ Jesus," must not confine himself to one sort of aliment: neither to *dogmata* alone, nor prophecies alone, nor promises, nor precepts, nor anything else, alone. The man of God, to be perfect, and thoroughly furnished unto all good works, must not only remember, but act upon it, that *all* Scripture is given by inspiration of God, and is profitable for doctrine, for reproof, for correction, for instruction in righteousness. (2 Tim. 3 : 16, 17.) No doubt we all fail here. Our faith does by no means compass the wide area of the Divine communications. Certain portions of the luxuriant field have a stronger claim upon it than others; but it might be useful to consider whether we reap from any single rood the yield which faithful tillage would bring out of it.

"Go to any particular parts of God's revelation —one and another—and say: Here is something for my faith—that is, for me to believe and be in a right manner affected by it. Has my faith ever been here? Has this really been taken within its compass? It is true, I did not discredit nor deny this—or this. But has it ever been to me that which the Divine Spirit wrote it here for? Has it been to me that instruction—impression—holy influence—for which it was designed? If not, then my faith has not extended to this; has not included it. And even now, is my faith acting upon it, or it upon my faith?—How often in such an exercise of trial, shall we find cause to repeat the prayer, 'Increase our faith'!"*

Here, according to the old, familiar theology, is the broad scope and legitimate function of faith in the work of sanctification: and it offers a significant contrast to the restricted agency assigned both to faith and to Divine truth, in the Higher Life scheme.

* Foster.

CHAPTER X.

THE LESSONS OF 1 JOHN, CHAPTER I.

RECURRING to the alleged efficacy of the act of consecration, as asserted by these writers, they have not produced, and cannot produce, a single inspired text which affirms that the believer may attain perfect sanctification by an instantaneous act of faith. Some of the principal texts which they interpret as of this purport, have been examined. It remains to notice one which, at the first glance, may seem to favor the speculation, but which can readily be shown to bear no such meaning. It has been reserved for this stage of the discussion because it must be viewed in its connection: and the Epistle in which it occurs, must be expunged from the Bible, before the notion of an earthly sinless life can be conceded.

The verse referred to is 1 John 3:9: "Whosoever is born of God doth not commit sin; for His seed remaineth in him: and he cannot sin because he is born of God." Let our Higher

Life friends frankly confess that they are as far as we are, from taking this verse literally. Taken thus, it asserts that *every* Christian lives without sin. Not merely eminent saints, not simply the "consecrated" who have learned the way of "practical holiness," but "whosoever is born of God." Every sinner rises to a state of sinless perfection at the moment of his regeneration! Of course they reject this notion: and in rejecting it, are forced to admit that the statement of the venerable apostle must be qualified by other Scriptures. The language clearly refers to habitual sin. The "seed" is the principle of grace or of the new life, implanted in the new birth; the principle which prompts to all holy obedience, and the absence of which is proved by the practice of wilful sin. He who thus sins, evinces that he is not born of God. Whereas, if to sin at all attests a man's unregeneracy, then have there never been, from the Ascension until now, any truly renewed souls; every one professing to follow Christ has been a child of the devil (v. 8: "He that committeth sin is of the devil"); and therefore the Gospel is an absolute failure. One need not waste words in vindicating the true interpretation of this passage.

But the beloved John has somewhat more to

say, a more sure word, whereunto they and we do well to take heed as unto a light that shineth in a dark place. For what is it we read in the first chapter of this Epistle?—" If we say that we have no sin, we deceive ourselves and the truth is not in us." And here we are confronted again with the peculiar canons of interpretation adopted by these authors. It would inevitably happen that many persons on reading or hearing one of their discourses, would instantly recur to the Scripture just quoted, and ask how the notion of an unsinning life could be reconciled with it. It is an obstacle so formidable, lying at the very threshold of the inner sanctum which all are invited to enter, that it cannot possibly be overlooked by any one familiar with the Scriptures. What have they done to help these doubters over it? In two instances only (so it is believed) have they noticed it, although the preceding verse reappears on all occasions. The passage runs thus: "If we walk in the light, as He is in the light, we have fellowship one with another, and the blood of Jesus Christ His Son cleanseth us from all sin. If we say that we have no sin, we deceive ourselves, and the truth is not in us. If we confess our sins, He is faithful and just to forgive us our sins and to cleanse us from all unrighteousness." Here, in one of the instances, the citation stops, and is thus expounded: "It is remarkable that right between the two passages, which more absolutely than any others in all the Scripture, declare the inward cleansing of the believer 'from all sin' and 'from all unrighteousness,' we find the warning against any claim to an inherent righteousness, any goodness in ourselves apart from the purifying influence of the blood of Christ, and the provision in case of failure for instantaneous pardon on the confession of our sin. That is: after we, as the children of God, have known divine fellowship in the light, and have been inwardly 'cleansed from all sin,' should so grievous an event occur as the revival of old evil in our hearts, with consequent trespass, the same instant in which the soul becomes conscious of sin, should also witness its free and full confession. Simultaneously with the knowledge of trespass and its confession, the soul should also realize God is faithful to His promises in having pardoned it. . . . Nor does this blessed word of promise stop here, but it carries the soul onward to the inward recleansing of the heart 'from all unrighteousness,' or from the internal taint, caused by a lapse of faith, from which the trespass proceeded. Thus the same flash of consciousness shall realize the sin—the confession—the forgiveness—and the soul-cleansing, all in a single instant of time." *

Short shrift this. Sin—confession—forgiveness—and perfect soul-cleansing—all comprehended "in the *flash* of consciousness," and completed "in a single *instant* of time." If this be scriptural, it is Scripture cast in a new mold. Is there no part of their scheme in which they can endure the element of contrition? The Bible enjoins repentance, and "confession" implies it. Repentance is godly sorrow for sin. What sort of repentance is that which is crowded, with three other very weighty elements, into "an instant of time"? Take the Concordance, and see whether the Bible anywhere recognizes a repentance which excludes all opportunity for serious reflection, penitential sorrow, and prayer. Is there no danger that those who follow this counsel may discover in the end, that their repentance was not "the repentance which needeth not to be repented of;" and that the peace which followed the "flash" of their "confession," was the delusive peace "which the world giveth"?

And why did the writer decline quoting the very next verse, unless from a latent suspicion that to cite it just then and there, would annul his

* *Walking in the Light.*

interpretation of the context? For how can that interpretation stand side by side with the emphatic declaration, "If we say that we have not sinned, we make Him a liar and His word is not in us"? In the other example in which the passage is explained,* this verse *is* added: but the quotation stops short in the middle of the ensuing verse, the first half of which is used for a purpose which the whole verse would frustrate. After saying that the passage teaches a cleansing, "not only from the stains of sin, or the punishment of sin, but from sin itself," he again applies it to the case of the fully sanctified who, having slipped, are instantly recovered and recleansed: thereupon "lest they should forget that they *had been* sinners, they are again reminded of the sorrowful fact (v. 10), but are at once told that these very things have been written us, 'that we sin not.'" (Chap. 2:1.) Whence this untoward propensity to cut texts in two? The residue of the verse shows that, after all, these very persons may still sin: "That ye sin not; and *if any man sin*, we have an Advocate with the Father, Jesus Christ, the righteous."

Here, then, is another passage of Scripture perverted from its obvious meaning, to make it sub-

* *Holiness through Faith.*

servient to the Higher Life theology. It is assumed without warrant, that the apostle is simply describing the experience of a believer who in v. 7 becomes *sinless;* in v. 8 yields momentarily to some temptation; but v. 9 confesses, is forgiven, and restored to his sinless condition, all "in a single instant of time." What does the apostle really say? He says (1) that the blood of Christ is efficacious to cleanse us from all sin, —which is the faith of the Church catholic, and the actual experience of all who have gone to their rest. (2) That "if *we*"—any of us—any believers whatever, irrespective of creed, sect, profession, experience—"if we say that we have no sin, that we are living without sin, and stand in no need of that precious blood, to cleanse us, not from the sin we may commit hereafter, but from the sin which defiles us *now*, we deceive ourselves, and the truth is not in us." And is not this the identical claim which is boldly asserted? I am now delivered (V. above) "not only from its stain and its punishment, but from sin itself"—which is tantamount to saying, "I have no sin:" nay, as another writer puts it, "I have even no *tendency* to sin!" (3) The apostle assures the penitent who confesses his sin, of God's readiness to pardon and purify him. But (4) however pardoned and purified, to deny his sin is "to make God a liar." The critics explain that v. 10 describes the concrete act, and v. 8 the abstract state: "The use of the perfect, 'have not sinned,' does not warrant an exclusive reference to sins anterior to conversion, but denotes active sinfulness reaching down to the present, and sins just committed: for it is of the sins of Christians the apostle is speaking, and what Christian would think of denying his *former* sins?"

We have here, then, a most solemn warning against any and every type of Perfectionism. The plain, incontrovertible import of the passage is, that the man is a SELF-DECEIVER who claims for himself, *what the apostle John dared not claim,* (for he speaks for himself as well as others, "If *we* say that *we* have no sin,") viz.: that he is now free from sin. Naturally enough, the evangelical commentators emphasize the lesson. The first paragraph below is from Scott. It is proper, in quoting it, to mention that the last sermon preached by this excellent man, (March 4, 1821,) was an exposition of the parable of the Pharisee and the Publican—a service which he closed with a very affecting application to *himself,* of the prayer, "God be merciful to me a sinner:"—"The apostle in this passage guards with as much care against self-righteous pride as against an Antinomian perversion of the Gospel. If any professed Christians, while they seemed to 'walk in the light,' should be so elated with a conceit of their own attainments as to say that they 'had no sin,' but were perfectly pure, and as holy in heart and life as the law of God required, they were certainly deceived in a most awful manner; nay, 'the truth was not in them, as a principle of life and illumination, or they never could have fallen into a mistake which implied gross ignorance of God, of His spiritual law, and of their own hearts." Again, the following passage from Braune's Commentary on the General Epistles of John (one of Lange's series) will find a response in the ordinary Christian consciousness; and if true, it shows the utter fallacy of the treatise entitled, "Walking in the Light:" "The certainty of the difference between walking in the darkness and walking in the light, is not greater than the certainty that those who are walking in the light have sin adhering to them. Vast as is the difference between these two modes and spheres of life, yet the import of the difference among Christians still affected with sin but experiencing a daily growing redemption from sin, vanishes before the purity of God the Father, no matter how marked and important the difference may be between a *John* and individual church-members. The perception and cognition of sin, especially of one's own sin, and the clear consciousness of it in all humility, are indispensable requisites for walking in the light. Though your sin, as compared with that of the unregenerate be light, take care lest you esteem it light. The smallest stain soils a clean garment. If you despise it when you weigh it, be afraid when you count it up. Many little sins make one great sin: many drops make a river." "We must not look for perfect holiness in this world. Those who entertain the fancy that they may be or are perfect, are like those who walk on stilts, or over precipitous cliffs: before they are aware of it, they will fall and come to naught." (*Starke.*)—"As it would be very vain and criminal in us to deny our having any sin, as it would be self-deceit to imagine it, and self-confusion to affirm it, let us with humble thankfulness apply to that blood which is able to cleanse us from all unrighteousness." (*Doddridge.*)

To these testimonies may be added another from a source which all Christian scholars will recognize as of the very highest weight. I quote from the exposition of Philippians by Mons.

Daillé, that illustrious ornament of the French Protestant Church.* He is commenting on chapt. 3 : 12–14 : "Not as though I had already attained, either were already perfect," etc.

"The opinion of our own perfection is a very dangerous error, and has two most pernicious consequences: the one renders us guilty of pride, the disposition of mind most at variance with salvation, God giving grace to the humble: the other relaxes the nerves of devotion. . . . If there ever had been any man in the world who could pretend to perfection, it would, without doubt, be this great apostle. . . . Yet after all his great combats, his glorious victories, his admirable triumphs, hear him saying with deep and heart-felt humility, 'Not that I have already apprehended, either am already perfect: no, brethren, I count not myself to have apprehended.' Who is there after this, sufficiently bold to speak of his supposed 'perfection'? Where is he who dares attribute to himself that which Paul confesses he had not? None, clearly, should be

---

* In the judgment of the writer, there is no commentary extant, except Leighton on 1st Peter, which is worthy to stand on the same shelf with *Daillé's Expository Lectures* on Philippians and Colossians. (Published by the Presbyterian Board of Publication.)

ashamed to acknowledge with him, that he sometimes fails. . . . Let us rest assured that the sanctification of the apostle, however excellent it might be, was not perfected in all points as long as he remained on the earth. From whence it follows, that no man living is perfected here below. This the Scriptures, the ancient Church, and our own consciences so loudly witness, that it is wonderful men can be found so deafened by the love of self that they hear none of these voices. Does not the Scripture tell us, that 'there is no man living who can be justified before God'? Why not, if there are some perfectly righteous? That every believer, though he were a confessor or an apostle, must thus pray *daily* to God, 'Forgive us our sins, as we forgive them that trespass against us'? Why thus, if there are some who never sin, and therefore need no pardon? Does it not say that 'in many things we all offend'? How so, if there are some faultless? Does it not say, that 'now we know but in part, and see through a glass darkly'? How so, if holiness, which is the fruit and effect of this sight, is not 'in part' but in perfection? Does it not say, that 'the flesh lusteth against the Spirit and the Spirit against the flesh, and that these are contrary the one to the other, so that we cannot do the things that we would'? But how can this be, if there are those who sin no more? Does it not say again, that 'if we say we have no sin, we deceive ourselves, and the truth is not in us'? Could it possibly say anything more express against this error? . . . Justly does Augustine say, that 'not one of the saints while he is in the body can possibly have every virtue; that there are none without sin; and none are *foolish or arrogant* enough to think they *need not say the Lord's Prayer* on account of sin, though in comparison with other men their sins may be few.' And further, 'He has greatly profited in that holiness during his life, which shall one day be perfected, who has discovered, as he advanced, his distance from the perfection of righteousness. It is by the wisdom, not by the impotence, of God that no believer is ever perfect here below; the Lord so conducting the saints in this life, that there should always remain something either to give them freely when they ask, or to pardon them mercifully when they confess to Him. The reason of this is hidden from us in the depth of His wisdom, in order that the mouth even of righteous men may be stopped in regard to their own glory, and may be opened only for the praise of God.' . . . Conscience also will confirm the testimony of Scripture and of the Fathers. . . . Whose flesh has at all times rendered a full and entire obedience to the dictates of the Spirit, without resisting His motions, without murmuring against His orders, without struggling against His illumination? If you make no inward war against this enemy, sin, how is it you are not ashamed! If you do, why not confess that you are not perfect? For certainly (as Augustine has said) it is either stupidity not to be aware of such palpable imperfection, or effrontery to deny it."

These quotations will bear to be supplemented by a brief passage from Marshall, on the respective moral tendencies of the two doctrines: "Perfectionists appeal to men's consciences to answer this question: Which doctrine is most likely to bring people to the practice of true godliness: theirs, which teacheth that perfect holiness may be attained in this life; or ours, which teacheth that it is impossible for us to keep the law perfectly, and to purge ourselves from all sin as long as we live in this world, though we use our best endeavors? They think that common reason will make the verdict pass for them against our doctrine, as that which discourageth all endeavors for perfection, and hardeneth the hearts of people to allow themselves in sin because they cannot avoid it. But on the contrary, the doctrine of Perfectionists hardens people, to allow themselves in sin, and to call evil good,—as the Papists account that the concupiscence of the flesh against the Spirit, is no sin, but rather good matter for the exercise of their virtues, because the most perfect in this life are not without it. It also discourageth those who labor to get holiness in the right way by faith in Christ, and maketh them to think that they labor in vain because they find themselves still sinful and far from perfection, when they have done their best to attain it. It hindereth our diligence in seeking holiness by those principles and means whereby only it can be found. Whatsoever good works the doctrine of the Perfectionists may serve to promote, I am sure it hindereth a great part of that work which Christ would have us to be employed in as long as we live in this world. We must know that our old state, with its evil principles, continueth still in a measure, or else we shall not be fit for the great duties of confessing our sins, loathing ourselves for them, praying earnestly for the pardon of them, a just sorrowing for them with a godly sorrow, accepting the punishment of our sins, and giving God the glory of His justice, and offering to Him the sacrifice of a broken and contrite spirit, being poor in spirit, working out our salvation with fear and trembling."*

It is not from any lack of direct Scripture testimony to the fallacy of the scheme we are examining, that these quotations are multiplied. (See James 3 : 2; Prov. 20 : 9; 1 Kings 8 : 46; Eccl. 7 : 20.) But candid readers of every name must concede that great deference is due to the views of sanctification adopted, after long and prayerful study, by such eminent Christian scholars—especially where they represent the leading Biblical critics of the Protestant world. We yield to the Higher Life school, the suffrages of the Pelagian and Roman Catholic Commentators, who argue in favor of perfect sanctification in this life; the former, on the ground that the soul received no serious damage by the fall; the latter, on the two-fold ground that baptism replaces our native corruption with inherent righteousness, and that we are thus enabled to render even a supererogatory obedience to the "mitigated law" of the new Dispensation. The contrast between these expositors and those who are held in merited honor in nearly or quite all the evangelical com-

* *On Sanctification* Direction xii.

munions, might well constrain the disciples of the new Perfectionism to re-examine its assumptions by the light of God's holy word. Certainly the ultimate appeal must be to that word, not to its expounders. But on the question, "What is really the teaching of Scripture on the subject of sanctification?" no serious-minded Christian will lightly contemn the concurrent authority of that great body of learned and devout interpreters, who stand by the doctrine which is incorporated with the ancient Creeds and Confessions. It is within the bounds of *possibility* that they may mistake herein the mind of the Spirit. But the thoughtful inquirer will pause when asked to discard their assistance in the study of the sacred oracles, in favor of teachers whose novel glosses upon familiar texts, have no vouchers but themselves. Can they be safe guides who say, "In so far as we know ourselves, *we have no sin*"; when an inspired apostle has said, " If we say that we have no sin, we deceive ourselves, *and the truth is not in us*"?

CHAPTER XI.

THE LAW DEBASED—SIN, NO SIN—THE LORD'S PRAYER.

It will naturally be asked, "What resource have the school we are dealing with, when pressed with Scripture texts, or arguments drawn from the Scriptures, which conflict so fatally with the notion of perfect sanctification?" The question has been incidentally answered: but so much stress is laid on the plea they present, that it demands a careful dissection. It so happened, that just before reaching this stage of the inquiry, a good Providence placed in the author's way a newspaper slip which in so far as it covers the ground, is equally candid, lucid, and effective. It summarizes much of the ground we have gone over, and will serve to introduce some additional observations. After referring to the inner life of certain eminent saints, the writer * proceeds thus:

"No matter how clearly they apprehend their present privileges in Christ, a sense of personal

* E. K. Alden, D. D.

sinfulness abides: and one of the most striking features of their richest Christian experience is, that it is *penitential.* Contrast with this another style of language which we sometimes hear: 'I love God with all my heart, and soul and mind and strength, and I love my neighbor as myself. I am conscious of no sin, and have not been thus conscious for a considerable time. Accordingly, I do not feel the need of confessing sin, or of praying for forgiveness. I confess weaknesses and imperfections, but not sinfulness; for of sinfulness I am no longer conscious; and with what may be below consciousness I have nothing to do.' One of the prominent characteristics of this experience is the lack of the penitential element. Consciousness of present ill-desert has ceased: it no longer cries, 'God, be merciful to me a sinner,' 'Cleanse thou me from secret faults.' What it calls its own 'consciousness of love, of entire consecration, of full surrender,' it is satisfied with, as personal holiness, needing itself no cleansing, no forgiveness. In other words, it lowers the standard of personal holiness to one's own consciousness of attainment, instead of retaining the divine standard 'holy as God is holy,' 'perfect as God is perfect,' 'pure as Christ is pure.' Some one has called this process, introducing 'a mitigated law suited to the debilitated standard of man.' It is a subtle method of retaining self-satisfaction while continuing in a state of sin. Instead of going through the seventh chapter of Romans into the eighth, as it thinks it is doing, it slips back unconsciously into the condition of being 'alive without the law,' refusing to test its own righteousness by God's perfect standard. Of course it is not conscious of sin; 'for by the law is the knowledge of sin.' Lower the standard of present personal holiness to your own present consciousness of loving God and man, and 'knowledge of sin' ceases, not because sin has ceased, but because the sinner refuses to test himself by God's test. This experience, therefore, is a subtle form of Antinomianism, more perilous because subtle. While in words it exalts the Gospel method of sanctification by faith in Christ, it practically undermines that method; for this faith, which must be continuous to be efficacious, includes the perpetual sense of personal ill-desert, accompanied by the perpetual entire reliance upon the righteousness of Christ. And the more clearly we discern the perfect standard, the sinless Christ himself, the more painful will be our consciousness that we come short of that standard. 'If I say I am perfect, my own mouth shall prove me perverse.' On the supposition that there is a sinless man on earth, so made by the Gospel method of sanctification through faith in Christ, the man himself will be the last person to know it, or proclaim it. His neighbors will make the discovery long before he makes it; for one of his daily mottoes is, 'In lowliness of mind let each esteem other better than themselves.' More emphatically to the end of life will he repeat the apostolic sentence, 'This is a faithful saying, and worthy of all acceptation, that Christ Jesus came into the world to save sinners; of whom I am chief.' His daily song will be—

'This is the hidden life I prize—
A life of penitential love.'"

Here is the secret of this lofty claim to perfect sanctification. Instead of bringing their experience up to the standard of the Divine law, the law is brought down to their experience. What they maintain is, not the familiar and cheering doctrine, that the sincere love and obedience of the Christian, however imperfect, will be accepted and even graciously rewarded for Christ's sake: but that their own love and obedience come up to the full requisitions of the new law, under which they are living. But suppose they misapprehend the extent of the law: does this misapprehension make sin to be no sin? Saul of Tarsus believed that he was obeying the law: "I verily thought with myself that I *ought* to do many things contrary to the name of Jesus of Nazareth." (Acts 26 : 9.) Was he therefore guiltless in persecuting the Christians? Let it be understood that a God of perfect holiness could not do less than require perfect holiness in His creatures. "Be ye perfect, as I am perfect." "Be ye holy, for I am holy." "Think of the absurdity there is in the idea that His law should require less than perfect holiness. For that, *less*, what would it be? What would or could the *remainder* be *after* holiness up to a certain point and stopping there? It must be *not* holiness, just so far. Not holiness? and what must it be then? What *could* it be but something *un*-holy, wrong, sinful? Thus a law not requiring perfect rectitude would, so far, give an allowance, a sanction, to what is evil—to *sin*. And from Him who is perfectly and infinitely holy!—an utter absurdity to conceive"! *

And consider what is involved in the idea, that God's law must flex and bend, to adapt itself to the capacities of different individuals and races.

* Foster.

Man's depravity makes him unable to obey a law requiring perfect holiness: then, according to this dictum, the law must exact of him only a very partial and precarious obedience, while it sanctions the whole iniquitous residuum, in his heart and life. The viler a sinner, the greater, of course, his disability; and therefore the less his obligation to obedience! What, then, is the measure of Satan's responsibility to the Divine law? Not only so, but the law, on the Higher Life principle, has no longer either uniformity or certainty. You take the gauge of it from your own consciousness. Your neighbor does the same. The law then is one thing to him and another thing to you; and while you are both "wholly sanctified," your relative holiness differs as do your views of the law. Is this what the apostle means when he says, "By the law is the knowledge of sin"? Doubtless it *is*—in the ethics of this school: for the dim sense they have of sin, could proceed only from their restricting the jurisdiction of the law to an extremely narrow area. And it furnishes also a solution of the enigma, that, to the eyes of ordinary observers, there is about as much diversity, in the comparative perfection (the solecism is unavoidable) of those who profess to have secured "the blessing," as there is among the pilgrims who travel on a lower plane. All are "perfect," —but each after his kind; that is, each according to his own apprehension of the law. No wonder that the types and grades of this "complete sanctification," are somewhat perplexing even to those who look upon their wholly sanctified neighbors with the largest charity, and shut their eyes to their failings wherever it is possible.

But consider this whole thing for a moment in its only proper light. THE LAW OF GOD: what is it but the transcript of His own glorious character? Not a mere collection of statutes; but the expression of His adorable perfections— the outshining of His immaculate holiness and awful Majesty. Not a legislative ordinance, uttering one voice in this sphere and another in that, and taking cognizance only of outward acts and words: but an august, immutable code, presiding over the endless diversities of character and condition, of action and passion, in millions of orbs, and reaching to the innermost chambers of every rational soul. It lays its hand of arrest upon the most subtle unchaste desire, upon the least uprising of vanity or pride, upon a tainted emotion, upon the exhaling of a sinful aspiration. Nay, it presides over your whole material and moral mechanism hour by hour, and with its self-registering and unerring pen, it makes record as well of what you leave undone, as of what you do; sets down in ineffaceable characters your every omission of duty, your every failure in keeping up your paramount and unintermitted regard for God's glory, your every default in the matter of continually loving your neighbor as yourself.—Such is the law of God in the merest rudimental conception which can be framed of it, with the inspired word open before us. It is of *this* law the Saviour says: "Think not that I am come to destroy the law or the prophets; I am not come to destroy, but to fulfil. For verily I say unto you, till heaven and earth pass, *one jot or one tittle* shall in no wise pass from the law till all be fulfilled. Whosoever therefore shall break one of these least commandments, and *shall teach men so*, he shall be called the least in the kingdom of heaven; but whosoever shall do and teach them, the same shall be called great in the kingdom of heaven." (Matt. 5 : 17–19.) And it is of this same law the apostle says, quoting from Deuteronomy, "Cursed is every one that continueth not in *all* things which are written in the book of the law to do them." (Gal. 3 : 10.) "Do we then make void the law through faith? God forbid: yea, we establish the law." (Rom. 3 : 31.) And so James: "Whosoever shall keep the whole law, and yet offend in one point, he is guilty of all." (2 : 10.) What hint is there in these passages, of a "milder law" as the code of the new dispensation?

But our Higher Life teachers, in common with errorists generally (see Ecclesiastical History at large) have no relish for a law like this. "We are not called to the standard of a different dispensation from that in which our lives are to be lived. We are not called to walk by the rule of angels who excel in strength, while we exceed all other creatures in weakness, nor even by the rule of the yet unfallen Adam. Neither is our standard that which will be ours in glorified bodies. . . . The obedience to which Christ is wooing us is not the legal obedience, a stainless perfection of knowledge and act impossible to these clouded faculties. That would indeed be an impossible and *grievous* command. 'If ye are led of the Spirit ye are not under law.' We are called to a hearty and supreme love of God, and to love our neighbor as ourselves. 'Love is the fulfilling of the law.' 'A new commandment I give unto you, that ye love one another, as I have loved you, that ye also love one another. . . . Jesus saith unto him, Thou shalt love the Lord thy God with all thy heart and with all thy soul and with all thy mind. . . . And thou shalt love thy neighbor as thyself. On these two commandments hang all the law and the prophets.'"*

This paragraph repeats, with immaterial variations, what was said years ago by the Rev. Charles G. Finney in the "*Oberlin Evangelist.*" It is a very frank avowal of the pernicious and irreverent doctrine, that it would be oppressive on God's part not to let His law down to the level of our capacities. But the attentive reader will observe that the disclaimer in the first part of the paragraph, is effectually annulled by the texts brought to sustain it at the close. We are not called (we read) to walk by the rule of angels, nor by that of Adam, nor by any rule which transcends our feeble powers: Christ has introduced a milder law, the law of love. Will the author kindly turn to the verse already quoted, Matt. 5 : 48, and say whether or not it was our blessed Lord who issued the command, and whether it is not addressed to us all : " Be ye therefore PERFECT even as YOUR FATHER which is in heaven is perfect"? Are the angels under a "higher rule"

* *Holiness through Faith.*

than this? Was Adam?—Then, again, the Saviour recognized and re-enacted the primitive law, when He resolved its ten commandments into two. Does He require of the angels that they should do *more* than love God "with all their hearts," and their fellows as they love themselves? Did He require more of Adam? And does He require less of us? What, then, becomes of the notion that we are under a law which does not require a sinless perfection?

A very curious and, it may be added, a very mischievous conception of law and sin, is that which runs through these books. "In speaking of sin here, I mean conscious, known sin. I do not touch on the subject of sins of ignorance, or what is called the inevitable sin of our nature, which are all covered by the atonement and do not disturb our fellowship with God. I have no desire nor ability to treat of the doctrines concerning sin: these I will leave with the theologians to discuss and settle, while I speak only of the believer's experience in the matter. And I wish it to be fully understood that in all I shall say, I have reference simply to that which comes within the range of our consciousness."* Here we have (1) a disavowal of any intention or

* *The Christian's Secret.*

capacity "to discuss the doctrines concerning sin," with an intimation that those are questions which appertain only to professed "theologians." Is this a mere class question, the nature of sin? Is its "nature" one thing to the theologian and another to the common Christian? Is it possible for any one to have right views of the remedy, without right views of the disease? And with what propriety can disclaimers of this sort be made by a writer who composes treatises, *ex professo*, on the way to get rid of sin, and, who, in doing that, could not and does not, avoid teaching "a doctrine concerning sin"? (2) We have here, as often elsewhere, the arbitrary restriction imposed upon the Divine law, which makes our consciousness the measure of its obligation. If we may thus limit the law as to its depth, why not as to its breadth also? If you may say, "I have no concern with sinful propensities or motions down in the unfathomed depths of my nature," why may you not say, "I will obey the first eight commandments, but I decline to acknowledge the obligation of the last two"? For it is not more certain that God has enacted the ninth and tenth precepts, than it is that He has imposed His law upon the most secret thoughts and intents of the heart. It is the imperative duty of every person carefully to watch against sin, and, when guilty of it, to repent and seek forgivness at the cross. But the lesson practically inculcated by this school, is, that if you avoid conscious sin, you may waive all apprehension as to your spiritual condition: your sanctification is complete. From a thousand facts which might be cited to expose the deluding tendency of the scheme, let it suffice to ask, How about that brand plucked from the burning and made a brilliant star in Christ's right hand, John Newton? For several years after his conversion, he continued to prosecute the slave-trade on the coast of Guinea. "He had not the least scruple as to the lawfulness of this traffic. He considered it as the appointment of Providence; and viewed the employment as respectable and profitable." Let him speak for himself: "I never knew sweeter or more frequent hours of Divine communion than in my *two last voyages to Guinea*, when I was either almost secluded from society on ship-board, or when on shore among the natives. I have wandered through the woods, reflecting on the singular goodness of the Lord to me in a place where perhaps there was not a person who knew me for some thousand miles around. Many a time upon these occasions, I have restored the beautiful lines of Propertius to their rightful Owner, and said :

> 'In desert woods with Thee, my God,
> Where human footsteps never trod,
>   How happy could I be!
> Thou my Repose from care, my Light
> Amidst the darkness of the night,
>   In solitude my company.'"

Here was a Christian living, in so far as the slave-trade was concerned, "without conscious sin." Was the traffic innocent because he thought it so? Did his "unconsciousness" of its criminality, save it from the malediction of God? Did the Divine law, in its requisition upon him, pause at the precise line where his "light" became darkness, and absolve him from all responsibility as to what lay beyond? This is a legitimate application of the Higher Life doctrine of sin to the case of John Newton. Nor let his name pass without again reminding those who may have embraced these views, of the deceitfulness of the heart. Newton's self-deception was frightful. But "as in water face answereth to the face, so the heart of man to man." We have none of us got beyond the lowest form in Christ's school, if we have not learned, each for himself, that "he that trusteth in his own heart, is a fool."

But they concede that the two great commandments are binding upon us; and with them must be taken the injunction, "Whether, therefore, ye eat or drink, or whatsoever ye do, do all to the glory of God." If, then, you are living "without conscious sin," either your "consciousness" must be very shallow, blind, and precarious, or *this* must be your condition, to wit: "Your supreme love to God burns with an undimmed radiance. It illumines, pervades, and controls your whole character. You carry about with you an abiding sense of His presence. You see God in everything and everything in God. You find your supreme happiness in the contemplation of His perfections. The fervor of your zeal for His honor knows no abatement. Your devotion never languishes. You are neither elated by prosperity nor depressed by misfortune. A paramount regard to His glory animates you in your eating and drinking, your buying and selling, your working and resting—in all your plans, all your reading, all your conversation, all your *feelings* as well as actions in every relation in life. You have 'brought into captivity every *thought* to the obedience of Christ.'

You have taken the measurement of the strongest principle of our constitution, that which pertains to us in common with the angels and all rational creatures, self-love, and you are able to say that you cherish for your neighbors the same intense love that you bear toward yourself. In your intercourse with them, you are a stranger to selfishness, to irritability, to petulance, to indifference. Their interest, honor, and comfort, are as dear to you as your own. You never regard them with an emotion of pride or self-sufficiency. You never talk of their failings. You never resent any injury they may do you. You always do to them as you would have them do to you. There is not one of them from whom you have withheld any friendly office which you might have rendered him: not one to whom you could not say on a casual meeting, 'My Brother—my Sister—I love you just as sincerely, just as ardently, as I love myself.'"

This is a faint adumbration of the demands which the "two great commandments" lay upon you. If you fall short in any of these particulars, you sin. And they are all such as *ought* to come within the sweep of an instructed "consciousness." It is neither said nor believed that the schedule exhausts the requisitions of the law:

but one should at least be able to affirm, that he is chargeable with neither transgression nor omission in so far as this summary goes, before he ventures to say, "I am living without conscious sin." Does some one despairingly reply: "If we are subjected to a law so rigorous as this, there is no hope for any of us:" the answer is two-fold. (1) There *is* no hope for us, through the law. "For what the law saith, it saith to them who are under the law, that every mouth may be stopped, and all the world may become guilty before God." (2) "Christ is the end (or fulfilling) of the law for righteousness to every one that believeth." "Where sin abounded, grace hath much more abounded." Our sins are great, but we have a greater Saviour. And, trusting in Him, our iniquities are blotted out; our poor sin-stained obedience and worship are accepted, for Christ's sake only—not because they satisfy the law's demands; and we receive constant supplies of grace, according to our various needs.—If, on the other hand, one presumes to say, "I shrink not from this test. I can charge myself with neither fault nor failure under any of the particulars which have been specified. I do love God with all my heart, and everything I do and say and feel, springs from a desire to glorify Him. I do love my neighbor just as much as I love myself, and all my words and actions attest it. My conscience is void of offence toward God and man. And it has been thus with me for months and years:"—If any one ventures to say this, instead of envying him his perfect sanctification, most Christians will regard him as entitled to the commiseration of every one who has learned the plague of his own heart. Better far to "live in the seventh of Romans" for a life-time, than to emerge into an intoxicating atmosphere which surrounds the pilgrim with optical illusions, and obscures all the landmarks that identify the King's highway.

Perfectionists of all schools have been embarrassed by the Lord's Prayer. The Higher Life writers, as is their custom with adverse Scriptures, rarely mention or even allude to it. In a single instance it is briefly touched upon, and the suggestion is made that the word "trespasses" means no more than "imperfections." Even if this were so, it would be pertinent to ask whether moral "imperfections" are compatible with a state of perfect sanctification. But this interpretation is not admissible. Turning to the Greek Testament, the word "debts" in Matt. 6: 12 is in v. 14 interchanged with "trespasses," and in Luke 11 : 4, with *sins*. To eliminate the idea of sin, is virtually to expunge the petition. To plead for forgiveness is to confess that you have sins to be pardoned. To offer this prayer daily—and such is the manifest design of the Saviour—is to confess that you sin daily. This is not to be conceded. A clergyman whose name has of late been much before the public, on applying, a year or two since, for admission into a Presbytery, was asked, " Are you in the habit of offering the Lord's Prayer?" "*Not for myself,*" he replied.* And such must be the answer of all the disciples of this faith, if they are true to their principles. Nothing startles people who are strangers to the system, more than this. They are slow to credit the announcement that there are any poor sinners this side of heaven, who have got beyond the Lord's Prayer. Were a person to appear amongst us who had really attained to this elevation, one to whom God had in His sovereignty given the Holy Spirit " without measure," and who was therefore able to lead such a life as an incarnate angel might lead, he would be an object of wonder and admiration to all beholders. But that in the absence of a miracle like this, there should be professing Christians who cannot pray, " Forgive

---

* This was told me by the pastor who proposed the question.

us our trespasses;" who can go daily to the throne of grace for weeks and months and even years, without having to confess a single sin,—it is no marvel that the statement should be met with the response—" If you are not, as you doubtless are, romancing, when you tell us of such cases, there is but one alternative: These persons are either imposing on your credulity, or they are the subjects of a profound self-delusion: the New Testament (like the Old) knows nothing of a religion for the sinless." There are no prayers in the Bible offered by unsinning believers. Daniel is generally regarded as an eminently holy man, standing perhaps at the very head, in this respect, of the Old Testament saints. See in his prayer (chap. 9) what he thinks of his own freedom from sin. Note Isaiah's prayer (chap. 64), and Jeremiah's (chap. 14) and the Psalmist's *passim*. Does any one imagine that David and Jeremiah, Isaiah and Daniel, would have scrupled about offering the petition day by day, " Forgive us our trespasses"? Can it be quite safe to venture, in our communion with the Deity, upon ground where these inspired men would not have dared to tread?

CHAPTER XII.

THE SCHEME INCOMPATIBLE WITH THE GENERAL TONE OF THE INSPIRED WORD—PILGRIM'S PROGRESS.

WE have thus far been treating of specific texts. There is another mode of testing the Higher Life doctrine—viz. by comparing it with the *general tone and complexion of the Sacred Scriptures.*—The restoration of man to the Divine image is, subordinately to the glory of God, the grand end and aim of Redemption. The various instruments and agencies ordained for giving effect to the work of Christ—the Scriptures, the Church and its ordinances, the Ministry, and the mission of the Spirit—all point to this result. It is intuitively certain that the means and methods of accomplishing it would be written as with a sun-beam upon the pages of the New Testament, would in fact be the burden of its teachings—as it really is. Now, according to our new guides, this august achievement is brought about by a single act of consecration. A simple volition to take Christ as your sanctification, makes you perfect in holiness; and, repeating this exercise of faith in Christ, you go on your way, sinning no more. You stand with the throngs of pilgrims at the base of the "Delectable Mountains," whose vertical crests are hid in the perennial bloom and beauty of the gardens outside the everlasting gates. How to reach that lofty plateau, is the engrossing question among you. In the midst of your amicable and helpful debates, you, all at once, put forth a volition in which you yield yourself up to Christ, and on the instant, *per saltum,* by a single bound, you scale the empyrean heights and find yourself revelling amidst the delights of the "Higher Christian Life," your sins vanquished, your burdens gone, your soul at peace, and your triumph complete. Your fellow-pilgrims pause in mute amazement as they witness the abrupt apotheosis—so abrupt, that they cannot see whether you drop your ar * or in your flight, nor learn whether you will have occasion for it in that celestial sphere. Some of them, newly entered upon the journey, may secretly envy your happy lot: while older travellers will be apt to say, one to another, "If the Lord of the City had intended that we should go up there, right on the face of the cliff, and quicker than a bird could fly to the top, He would surely have put up finger-posts to show us the way, or made it so plain in the chart He has given us, that more than one in a thousand would have discovered the path. We may as well keep to the old road."

Certain it is, that John Bunyan, who is commonly supposed to have had some acquaintance with the route, never suspected the existence of any such approach to the City of the Great King. If he had, the world would have missed one of the three books in the English tongue which are destined to live as long as the language itself lives. The path revealed to the glorious Dreamer, as he lay in Bedford jail, was well defined by its landmarks,—the Interpreter's House—the Lions—the Hill Difficulty—Vanity Fair—the Valley of the Shadow of Death—the Enchanted Ground—the Living Springs—Giant Grim—Doubting Castle—and so on to the Delectable Mountains, with the Land of Beulah in the distance. No "short-cut" for pilgrims, but a well-beaten path over hill and dale, through meadows, forests, jungles, and rivers—among rocks and thorns, fruits and flowers—through festal scenes and scenes of sorrow—with many a conflict—many a wound—but always certain victory—ever tending upwards—and an assured arrival at the final rest—a rest all the sweeter by reason of the toils and dangers of the way. Shut up in his prison with the study of the inspired chart as his only occupation, and the Divine Spirit as his only Teacher, Bunyan could find no path but this for pilgrims bound heaven-ward. And, by no strange coincidence, it is the path which most pilgrims, before and since his day, have found there. This fact makes it clear to demonstration, that the New Testament in its obvious meaning, is *adapted* to give this impression of the Christian life. It is so written that, century after century, the great mass of believers, to say nothing of learned and godly theologians, have understood it as teaching, that the Christian life is essentially a life of conflict within and without, and of progressive sanctification.

Now consider how utterly incongruous to the whole complexion of the New Testament, is this theory of perfection. Here everything centres in a single voluntary act of the soul. To that, everything points; from it, everything proceeds. Its tremendous importance no language can well exaggerate. It marks a transition approximating closely to that of the new birth itself. Until this line is passed, the Christian is leading a " Christ-dishonoring life." On one side of it he is in chains, on the other a freeman. On one side a servant, on the other a child. On one side there is anxiety, travail, struggle, drudgery; on the other, peace, serenity, joyousness, a sinless breast, an unclouded sky, and the conqueror's song. A transformation so mighty must needs be signalized by the sacred penmen, with a distinctness commensurate with its magnitude. It is with no uncertain sound and in no merely incidental way, they speak of human depravity, the atonement, justification, regeneration, faith, repentance. These topics stand out in such bold relief that they arrest the attention of the most casual reader. But here is an alleged feature of the Divine economy, of co-equal gravity—an act by which the Christian rids himself of his body of sin, and passes instantaneously into a condition of perfect sanctification, "the holiness of Christ becoming really his own." This pregnant step is no obligation or prerogative of a favored few. It is the imperative duty and high privilege of every disciple; so much so, that he who holds back from it, contents himself with a very unworthy style of piety, and grievously fails in his loyalty to Christ. Will its advocates have the kindness to point out in what part of the sacred record it is defined? Just where are we told of an act of "consecration" which constitutes the sum and core of true godliness? We do not want your inferences and speculations. We demand a "Thus saith the Lord," in support of your dictum, that a Christian, by putting forth a volition to "consecrate" himself to Christ, may thereby escape all further trouble from his inward corruptions, and enter upon an unsinning life. If the doctrine be true, the New Testament, which has sanctification for one of its two all-pervading themes, must be full of it: it must necessarily give coloring to the entire book. There is nothing which the Saviour so much presses upon His followers, nothing which the apostles so importunately pray for and so urgently inculcate in their Epistles, as the sanctification of believers. If it be so, that personal holiness is to be achieved by a single movement of the soul,* the most explicit directions must be given as to the duty and method of its accomplishment. This consecrating act, as not only ensuring the believer a release from the worst part of his present warfare, but placing

---

* The word "achieved" is used advisedly, for we are most strangely told, "the one Rest, from the guilt of sin, Jesus *gives* to the weary burden-bearer; the second is *found* by the meek and lowly yoke-bearer."— *Walking in the Light.*

him in a position where, instead of striving and working and wrestling, he will have but one solitary duty to perform—viz. to lie passively in Christ's hands and let Him "do it all"—this act must inevitably hold a most conspicuous position on the inspired page. For, as interpreted to us, it largely supersedes any necessity for specific exhortations and warnings. What occasion for caution or counsel, as to this or that danger, this or that sin, this or that duty, to one of whom the Lord Jesus Christ has, in His own *Person*, taken such absolute possession, that He prompts, directs, and controls all his willing and doing precisely as an idiot child is governed by its keeper? The Master may be safely left to look after the holiness of a disciple with whom He is *thus* identified. All the more certain is it, that the consecrating act itself, big with these momentous and blessed consequences, will be held up in every possible light, illustrated to the humblest capacity, and enforced with such affluence and cogency of argument as the Divine Spirit alone could supply. *Has this been done?* If so, tell us where. Point to the passages of God's word in which this pretended, all-potent "consecration," fills the central place assigned to it in your system—or, in fact, any place at all. The only verse which will be likely to suggest itself in response to this demand, is that in which Paul records his deliverance in the seventh of Romans. And, as we have seen, this prop breaks down as a Higher Life auxiliary, the moment the closing half of the verse is quoted: "So then with the mind I myself serve the law of God, but with the flesh *the law of sin.*" And further, we find him recognizing, in his Epistle to the Galatians, the same old conflict between the flesh and the Spirit; and with beautiful humility writing to the Philippians from his Roman prison, "Not as though I had already attained, either were already perfect." Paul is a poor witness for any scheme of perfection in this life. And we must still call for proof that the New Testament, either in its general tenor or in particular texts, makes the whole matter of personal religion, with its wide complexity of hopes, joys, duties, and privileges, to turn upon an instantaneous exercise of faith put forth by one who has already experienced renewal and forgiveness.

CHAPTER XIII.

A BLEAK SYSTEM FOR DOUBTING AND DESPONDING BELIEVERS.

In certain of the books we are examining there are chapters entitled, *"A Wavering Faith"* —*"Doubts"*—*"Failures."* The admission is freely made, that even the fully consecrated do sometimes "waver;" that they lapse into "doubt;" and temporarily "fail." This is no strange thing, and, to an observer, is rather a hopeful sign than otherwise. For an assurance which rests upon such a basis of quicksand as freedom from sin, ought to give way now and then to a healthful doubt. The counsels addressed to them, however, are of quite another tenor—coincident, indeed, with the instructions given at an earlier period on the subject of "consecration." The chapter on "Doubts," in the *"Christian's Secret,"* is written with a slashing pen. One who is even slightly acquainted with the voluminous literature of this subject, will stand aghast at the imperious tone which pervades it. If its utterances be drawn from the word of God, such books as Bolton's "*Cure for Afflicted Consciences,*" Rogers on "*Trouble of Mind,*" Colquhoun on "*Spiritual Comfort,*" Goodwin's "*Child of Light walking in Darkness,*" Sibbs's "*Bruised Reed,*" Jones's "*Man Physical and Moral,*" and many others of the kind, need never have been written. It is easy to imagine the amazement with which godly men like these, who had made the doubts and difficulties of believers a life-study, and, with learned skill and unwearied patience, explored every part of Holy Scripture bearing upon the subject, would have listened to the instructions here given to the halting, and the summary style in which their misgivings are disposed of: "Most Christians have settled down under their doubts, as to a sort of inevitable malady. They lament over them *as a man might lament over his rheumatism,* making themselves out as an 'interesting case' of especial and peculiar trial, which requires the tenderest sympathy and the utmost consideration. . . . One after another they fight with every declaration and every promise our Father has made to His children, and refuse to believe them, until they can have some more reliable proof of their being true, than the simple word of their God. And then they wonder why they are permitted to walk in such darkness, and look upon themselves almost in the light of martyrs, and groan under the peculiar spiritual conflicts they are compelled to endure. Spiritual conflicts! Far better would they be named, did we call them spiritual rebellions. . . . Just as well might I join in with the laments of a drunkard, and unite with him in prayer for grace to endure the discipline of his fatal appetite, as to give way for one instant to the weak complaints of these enslaved souls, and try to console them under their slavery. To one and to the other I would dare to do nothing else but proclaim the perfect deliverance the Lord Jesus Christ has in store for them, and beseech, entreat, command them with all the force of my whole nature, to avail themselves of it and be free. . . . From the beginning to the end of your Christian life, it is always sinful to indulge in doubts. *Doubts are all from the devil, and are always untrue.*"

Rough surgery this! It recalls the case of an eminent Philadelphia Surgeon, long before the days of Anæsthetics, who used to cut and carve upon his patients as if they were logs of oak. Here is a stout, robust nature, armored with an indefeasible assurance, and clearly a stranger to the class of disciples of whom it is written, "A bruised reed shall He not break, and smoking flax shall He not quench." It is no sin for one so unlike them, not to be able to comprehend such disciples. But to describe them in terms which border upon gross caricature; to treat their scruples with harsh irony; to tell them that all their doubts are rebellions inspired by the devil; and that, like would-be martyrs, they are invoking a sympathy which they do not deserve;—this is vivisection with a witness. And the hand which thrusts in the knife among the quivering nerves and tendons, is held by one who "commits no conscious sin"! Well, after large experience with these doubting Christians, some of whom were loved and revered by all who knew them as enrobed by the Spirit of God in His richest garniture, it is not improper for the author to say, that he would much sooner send them for counsel to a physician of the lower plane, like Flavel, or Fuller, or Alexander, than to one of the higher plane who could not prescribe the antidote for such maladies, except with an unsparing severity. Shall we assume to be wiser or more faithful than our blessed Master in dealing with these timid disciples? We have His methods portrayed both prophetically and experimentally. Some of His sheep are very weak, and given to wandering—oftentimes because, though they hear His voice, they cannot believe that He cares for, and is calling to, *them.* How does He treat them? "I will seek that which was lost, and bring again that which was driven away, and will bind up that which was broken, and will strengthen that which was sick." (Ezek. 34 : 16.) It was, indeed, a main part of His errand, "to preach good tidings to the meek, to bind up the broken-hearted, to proclaim liberty to the captives, and to appoint unto them that mourn in Zion, beauty for ashes, the oil of joy for mourning, and the garment of praise for the spirit of heaviness." (Isa. 61 : 1–3.) Accordingly, when He came, He had many of these "doubters" to deal with. To one of them He said: "O thou of little faith, wherefore didst thou doubt?" To another: "Reach hither thy finger and behold my hands, and reach hither thy hand and thrust it into my side; and be not faithless, but believing." The doubts of these and others of their class *may* have "come from Satan," and if so Jesus knew the fact: but He did not see fit to upbraid them with it. (Let it be added in a parenthesis, that the passage quoted above, which has given occasion to these comments, suggests some rather perplexing questions as to the sort of "consciousness" it is, which so attenuates sin that it detects nothing amiss in that style of dealing with the spiritual troubles of sincere Christians. Bring the law down low enough, and a good many people who now eschew the notion, may at least fancy that they too can live " without sin.")

It is not intended, by these remarks, to encourage Christians in doubting. There is far too much of doubting, and far too little of taking God at His word. It is sound advice, too, to bid the wavering disciple cast himself anew at the Saviour's feet, and embrace Him as his all-sufficient and all-willing Deliverer. Better still if a word or two had been added, reminding the hesitating soul, that the only way to return to Christ and recover peace and comfort, is, to pray earnestly for the enlightening, strengthening aid of the HOLY SPIRIT. There are passages in these books in which our dependence upon the Spirit, is distinctly recognized. But it is another of the untoward silences already noticed, that the three chapters written expressly to instruct doubting and drooping Christians how to regain their lost assurance, give no prominence whatever to the offices of the Divine Spirit. The chief reference is one which might better have been omitted—as follows: "The Holy Spirit never suggests a thought of doubt or discouragement to any soul. Never! Settle this matter once for all, and you will find the way wonderfully cleared." This is a specimen of the oracular style of utterance which we so often encounter. The sentiment here propounded as an axiom, cannot and will not be received without proof. The presumption is altogether the other way. It is in the highest degree probable, as regards Christians who have become remiss, and suffered their graces and their comfort to decline, that the compassionate Spirit does sometimes come to them in His loving faithfulness, and stir up a wholesome doubt in their breasts as to the validity of their hopes. That Christians in these circumstances are very apt to doubt, will not be denied. Would it not be more like " the father of lies" to lull such people into a deeper slumber than to arouse them to inquire into their evidences? Was it from *that* quarter such warnings as these came?—" Awake, thou that sleepest, and arise from the dead, and Christ shall give thee light." (Eph. 5 : 14.) " Examine yourselves, whether ye be in the faith; prove your own selves." (2 Cor. 13 : 5.) " Be watchful, and strengthen the things which remain, that are ready to die: for I have not found thy works perfect before God. Remember, therefore, how thou hast received and heard, and hold fast, and repent." (Rev. 3 : 2, 3.) All these, it is plain, were Christian professors who were thus admonished that they had *reason* to "doubt." What, then, becomes of the reiterated and deceptive aphorism, that "all doubts are from Satan"?

Their treatment of this topic supplies a fresh illustration of the point, that the "consecrating act" is the axle upon which the entire scheme revolves. Religious doubt and depression assume multiform shapes—taking their type from constitutional temperament, disease, education, knowledge of the Scriptures, home-life, and various other agencies. Questions like the following have been often asked: "How shall we know whether our faith is saving, amidst all the weaknesses and doubts that may attend it?" "What is the essential difference between a natural and a spiritual faith?" "May hope, love, repentance, patience, etc., evidence that a person is regenerated, although he is in doubt about the truth of his faith?" "Is it not presumptuous for a person to hope he has an interest in Christ, when he sees little or nothing in himself, but reason to doubt and question it?" "Whether a person may desire the blood of Christ to be applied to his soul, and yet be a hypocrite

"Can I have any right whatever to think that I am a child of God, when my conscious unfitness makes me shrink from going to the Lord's Table?" This is a mere sample of the questions with which Christian casuists are plied; and it requires a large knowledge of the old nature and the new, of the human heart, the word of God, and the ministry of the Spirit, to answer them satisfactorily. It would simplify matters immensely to be able to say to each one of these anxious souls: "As true as you live, your doubts proceed from the devil. Instantly consecrate yourself to Christ; and then assume that He has received you. Believe that you *do* believe, whether you can feel it to be so or not. Keep saying to yourself, 'I do believe, I do believe; Christ has said it, and it must be so. I *am* dead to sin. I *am* fully sanctified. I dare not doubt more.'"—In medicine, the indiscriminate use of a single prescription passes under the name of quackery. How utterly it would fail in casuistical theology, must be too apparent to require argument. There is no department of theology which demands greater skill; no function of the religious teacher, the exercise of which involves higher responsibility. Nor is it less certain that such advice as the above, so administered, would, in very numerous instances, entirely fail of its end. One class of burdened inquirers would listen to it with the feeling: "This leaves me more in the dark than ever." With another, an attempted compliance might possibly operate in this way: "I can and do make the effort to consecrate myself to Christ. I do not distrust His willingness to receive every sinner who comes to Him. But to believe in Christ is one thing: it involves a looking out of one's self, and a surrender of the whole heart, to the Saviour. To believe that I do thus believe in Him, requires me to *look within* and learn the character of my own exercises. Here I pause: for I know how blind we are to ourselves; how easily we mistake our own mental and moral condition; how liable to be self-deluded. To say to myself, 'I do believe,' does not make it so. Thousands have said this, whose eyes were speedily opened to discover their mistake. Many have, as they supposed, taken this step of consecration, and, thereupon, confidently 'reckoned themselves to be effectually dead unto sin and alive unto righteousness;' who nevertheless have presently learned that the law of sin in their members, though shorn of its supremacy, was still active. I must have surer ground to go upon, than *faith in my own faith*. All the more so is this the case when I am told :* 'There is one step absolutely necessary before you can possibly take any other. You must get on believing ground again, before you can again believe; and this ground is that of entire consecration to God.' Here I am instructed that I 'cannot believe until I get upon the believing ground of entire consecration.' How I am to get there *without* 'believing,' does not appear. To say, as is said in this sentence, that 'entire consecration to God,' is something which must *precede* the exercise of faith is, to my poor intelligence, equivalent to telling me,—'You must not touch pen and paper, until you have written your note.' And yet, after being thus admonished of the impossibility of exercising faith prior to consecration, and being told elsewhere by the same author, that 'full consecration is to be *received by faith*'†— after listening to these discordant voices, I am still reminded, that in order to regain my peace of mind, it is 'absolutely necessary' for me to 'believe that I *do* believe.'

'Here's a maze trod, indeed,
Through forth-rights and meanders! By your patience,
I must needs rest me.'"

* *Walking in the Light*, p. 30.
† *The Christian's Secret*, pp. 41, 45, etc.

It were no strange thing if many a lapsed believer should fall into this bewilderment, in attempting to escape from his doubts and fears, after the Higher Life method;—a reflection not in the least invalidated by the examples adduced of persons who are reported to have tried it successfully. It will be in order to use that argument, after it shall have been shown, that all doubters are alike, and require the same treatment; and that the treatment we have been analyzing, is that enjoined by the great Physician.

It is not sufficiently considered by the expounders of this system, that God exercises the same sovereignty in the spiritual as in the natural world. In either realm, to one he gives five talents, to another two, to another one, according to His good pleasure. No less by His Spirit than by His providence does He lead His people in diverse paths. One He endows specially with this grace; another with that. To one He reveals more of the depths of depravity in his own heart; to another, more of the unsearchable riches of Christ. One discerns the holiness of the Divine law, with a clearness which almost overwhelms him; another, the ineffable grace and mercy of the Gospel, with a fulness which ravishes him. One is panoplied with the active virtues; another, embellished with the passive graces. One has the faith of Abraham; another, the faith of Thomas. One is a *Great-heart* who rather enjoys meeting the lions and Giant Grim; another, a *Mr. Fearing* who "is dejected at every difficulty," and "carries a Slough of Despond in his mind." All these and many others are found among the bands of pilgrims who are traversing the narrow way. We are in no position to say, that the master-spirits among them, the resolute, the energetic, the exultant, who step as if they were already treading the golden streets, display the royal *insignia* one whit more unmistakably than some of their fellows who steal along with downcast eyes, looking as if they thought they might be arrested for trespassing upon that sacred thoroughfare. Very full they are of misgivings; and sadly deficient in that imperial faith for which they are secretly longing. What they think of themselves, comes out in all their approaches to the great God. "And now I that am but dust and ashes, have taken upon me to speak unto God." "I am more brutish than any man." "I abhor myself in dust and ashes." "Yet the dogs eat of the crumbs." "All our righteousnesses are as filthy rags." "God be merciful to me a sinner." This is their habitual strain in drawing near to the mercy-seat. But every eye except their own is attracted to a jewel they wear, one of the choicest of the crown jewels, which sheds its gentle radiance around them as they walk. It is much lauded in the inspired writings: "Though the Lord be high, yet hath He respect unto the lowly." "He giveth grace unto the lowly." "The ornament of a meek and quiet spirit, which is in the sight of God of great price." "Blessed are the poor in spirit, for theirs is the kingdom of heaven."

If there be any one distinctively Christian grace, it is this of *humility* which adorns the "bruised reeds;" for it is farther removed than any other grace from man's native disposition. Jeremy Taylor says of it: "Humility is the great ornament and jewel of the Christian religion; that whereby it is distinguished from all the wisdom of the world; it not having been taught by the wise men of the Gentiles, but first put into a discipline and made part of a religion, by our Lord Jesus Christ, who propounded Himself imitable by His disciples so signally in nothing as in the twin-sisters of meekness and humility: 'Learn of me, for I am meek and humble; and ye shall find rest unto your souls.'"* Of course this grace has its counterfeits. "A legal spirit is a more subtle spirit than many persons imagine. A spirit of pride as to our faith, humility, affections, experience, righteousness, or holiness, is a legal spirit. Every man who is lifted up by an elevated opinion of his experience, trusts in that experience, and makes a righteousness of it,— whatever humble language he may use with respect to himself, and though he attribute his discoveries to the operations of Divine grace, and even call upon others to glorify God for them. . . . There is a professed deadness to the law, which is one of the proudest things in the world; a humility which, to use very improper terms, is a confident, showy, assuming humility. It appears to be the nature of spiritual pride, to make professors ostentatious with respect to this grace. To be truly emptied of self; to be poor in spirit; to be broken in heart; is quite another thing, and has quite other effects from what is often supposed. It is astonishing to observe, how many are deceived about themselves in imagining that they are very humble when they are very proud, and their behavior very haughty. . . . Such is the nature of grace that it disposes the saints to

* *Holy Living*, chap. II.

regard their goodness as little, and their imperfections as great. Those who possess the most grace, possess likewise the most of this disposition. To a gracious soul, and especially to one eminently gracious, his holiness appears little in comparison with the obligations under which he is laid. As grace increases, this view extends itself until the soul is swallowed up by the vastness of the obligation, and astonished at the small degree in which this obligation is discharged. Deeply affected by the smallness of his attainments, he can scarcely conceive that anything similar has occured in the experience of other saints. It is amazing to him that a child of God, one who has actually received the unspeakable benefits of the amazing love of Christ, should love no more; and he is disposed to regard this circumstance as peculiar to himself—a strange and solitary instance of insensibility and ingratitude.". . . "The tendency of high religious affections in some persons with whom I have been acquainted, is to hide the depravity of their hearts, and to leave them without complaint as to the remains of moral depravity. A real saint (as has been shown) may know that he possesses true grace; and the more grace he possesses, the more easily may he arrive at this important knowledge.

But still it does not follow that an eminent saint is particularly sensible that he is an eminent saint compared with others. I will not deny that he who possesses much grace and is eminently holy, may know that he is thus distinguished; but it will not be obvious to him that he is better than others, so that this supposition should become a foremost thought—a something which from time to time, readily occurs to his mind. It may be remarked as infallibly true, that the person who upon comparing himself with others, is apt to think himself a very eminent saint, much distinguished in Christian experience; and in whom this is a leading thought, often recurring, is certainly mistaken. . . . A truly eminent saint is not disposed to think himself eminent in anything: all his experience and graces appear to him comparatively small, especially his humility. There is nothing belonging to his experience so much out of sight as this grace." *

These profound views come to us clothed with the authority of "the great metaphysician of the Eighteenth Century," whose still greater distinction it is, that he "walked with God," as a little child with its father. No uninspired man has displayed greater skill in dissecting the human

* *Edwards on the Affections*, Part III.

heart. In dealing with the abstruse problems growing out of the co-existence of sin and grace in the renewed man, he stands upon the high level of the chief Puritan divines. And while no infallibility is claimed for his judgment, those who, on a topic like that just presented, dissent from one so clearly taught of God, should be able to produce strong reasons in support of their opinions.

Now to apply Edwards's principles,—that genuine humility which he takes so much pains to discriminate from its counterfeits, is not unfrequently found in connection with painful "doubts" as to one's acceptance with God. Such doubts may spring from disordered nerves, from prejudices of education, from wrong instruction, from inadequate views of the covenant of grace, from mistaking vile thoughts injected by Satan for their own sins, from distrusting the Divine promises, from a morbid habit of scrutinizing and trying to analyze their own exercises. Whatever their source, these misgivings are still blended with tenderness of conscience, a deep sense of personal ill-desert, a longing for the light of God's countenance, and a faithful devotion to His service. If the *true* higher life be a life of love, of patience, of submission, of purity, of benevolence, of meekness, of watchfulness, of prayer, of helping the needy, consoling the afflicted, visiting the fatherless and widows, and promoting the happiness of all around, this life has been led by some who have been left for years in more or less of uncertainty as to their spiritual state. That they grievously erred in not appropriating to themselves the privileges of the new covenant; that unbelief was, more than anything else, the source of their troubles; will not be disputed. But to say to a Christian of this sort: "Consecrate your *doubts* to Christ. *Believe* that he *does* receive you. Reckon yourself to be a Christian, yea a fully sanctified Christian. Enter at once upon the life of practical holiness; and go on your way rejoicing:"—to say this, albeit embracing (by implication) the "one thing needful," of going to Christ and trusting in Him without delay, would be about as effective as to say to a north-western gale, "Peace: be still." No such stereotyped counsel thus curtly proffered, will suit these desponding souls. Nor, indeed, is it proper in any case to instruct a wavering disciple, that his paramount duty is to "renew his consecration," and then to assume that the prime function of his faith is to "believe that he does believe." This may, in some instances, bring peace, true or false, lasting or evanescent. But there is "a more excellent way;" and it consists in treating each case of spiritual doubt and difficulty according to its own symptoms, and with remedies derived from the inexhaustible treasury of God's word.

CHAPTER XIV.

THE SCHEME DEFICIENT IN SOLID COMFORT FOR GOD'S CHILDREN — SELF-DECEPTION — EGOISM.

WE advance a step farther in the same general direction, in charging that the Higher Life scheme is *sadly deficient in its provision for the security and comfort of believers.* This is not said in ignorance of what is claimed for it, as knocking off the Christian's chains and making him a free man. The system must be tested, not by its pretensions, but by the law and the testimony. That it is peculiarly conducive to self-deception has been incidentally pointed out in various connections. It has been justly observed, that "the notion of the actual attainment, in some instances, of perfect virtue in this life, is so gratifying to human pride, that we need not wonder at its adoption by some in nearly every age of the world. Contrary as it is to Scripture and experience, it is too deeply radicated in man's selfishness, not to find apologists and advocates among the conceited, the enthusiastic, and such as are unaccustomed to an impartial scrutiny of their own hearts. It flatters exceedingly all those pretensions to superior sanctity, which are disjoined from humility, penitence, and ardent aspirations after entire assimilation to the perfection of the Divine moral character."* The Higher Life school, therefore, make their appeal to a native and vivid susceptibility. They say to Christians of every name and grade: "It is your bounden duty and your sacred privilege, to rise, not in the future, but at once, to a state of moral perfection. The method is very simple. Consecrate yourself unreservedly to Christ. Then *believe* that you have taken Him as your sanctification, and that He has received you: and you have now entered upon the life of practical holiness."—More tersely thus: "The way is just as simple and plain as it is possible for a way to be. Desire; ask; believe that you receive; and you shall have. And then, having believed, never suffer yourselves to doubt again." † There is something very captivating in this summary method of getting rid of sin. No wonder that it *takes*. But how apparent is it, that in repre-

* *Princeton Review*, vol. xiv. 426.
† *The Christian's Cry*, p. 14.

senting it as so simple an affair, no account is made of man's self-ignorance; of his inability to control his affections by a mere volition; and of his disposition to regard the peace and complacency which follow his attempted consecration, as being necessarily derived from Christ! One might have supposed, that in setting forth the nature of this momentous step, the writers would multiply cautions against self-deception. But, as so often observed, the unmeasured deceitfulness of the heart, if a factor at all in the theory, is a very inefficient one.

"What, then!" it may be asked; "do you mean to affirm that all those who claim to have reached an unsinning state, are self-deceived?" It is not for man to read either his own heart or the heart of his fellow. But it is no unheard-of phenomenon that a Christian should think more highly of himself than he ought to think. As the Bible has been understood by the great mass of sincere believers, a claim to perfect holiness on the part of any sinner in this life, is, a *felo-de-se*; it destroys itself. To assert it, is to claim to be better than Abraham or Moses, Daniel or Isaiah, Nehemiah or Ezra, Paul or John. And people of average intelligence and candor, must be excused for not being able to see how this can be. "If we say we have no sin, we deceive ourselves." It seems undeniable, that every step the Christian takes upward, the nearer he approaches to the awful holiness of the Deity, the more certainly will it have the effect upon him which his vision of the Divine glory had upon the prophet. (Isa. 6.) Instead of dilating upon what grace has enabled him to achieve, he will be clothed with the deepest humility; and his feeling will be, "Unclean, unclean! for mine eyes have seen the King, the Lord of Hosts." It were easy to fortify this view by innumerable testimonies. Let one suffice from the pen of one of the holiest men (by consent of all Christian scholars) the Church militant has known from the Day of Pentecost until now. Referring to Archbishop Leighton, Burnet says: "He had the greatest elevation of soul, the largest compass of knowledge, the most mortified and most heavenly disposition, that I ever yet saw in mortal. He had the greatest parts as well as virtues, with the perfectest humility, that I ever saw in man. He had a sublime strain in preaching, with so grave a gesture, and such a majesty, both of thought, of language, and of pronunciation, that I never saw a wandering eye when he preached. I have seen whole assemblies often melt in tears before him. And I can say of him with great truth, that in a free and frequent conversation with him, for above two-and-twenty years, I never knew him say an idle word, or one that had not a direct tendency to edification: and I never once saw him in any other temper, but that which I wished to be in, in the last moments of my life. For that pattern, which I saw in him, and for that conversation, which I had with him, I know how much I have to answer to God; and though my reflecting on that which I knew in him, gives me just cause of being deeply humbled in myself, and before God; yet I feel no more sensible pleasure in anything than in going over in my thoughts all I saw and observed in him."

Well—in commenting on Ps. 130:3, "If Thou, Lord, shouldest mark iniquities, O Lord, who shall stand?" Leighton says: "He who on looking within does not see the sum and bulk of his sins to be immensely great, is either almost blind, or lives abroad, and never descends into his own breast. Give me the *holiest man upon earth*, the man who, above all others, stands at the remotest distance, both in the affections of his mind and the conduct of his life, from those sins which are acknowledged as mortal, will he not deeply feel his need of *daily* forgiveness, from the multiplied pollutions of his daily infirmities? Gross offences alone strike the eye of our fellow-creatures; but when we seriously consider that we have to do with an All-seeing Judge, who looks at once through every covering, and sees the most secret recesses of our hearts, who considers not only what may be concealed from men, but even what is concealed from ourselves, so as most clearly to discover even the least stain and speck of our inmost soul, and whose infinite holiness must also abhor it; is it possible that any one should be so infatuated as, in such a view, still to retain a false and foolish conceit of his own innocence? It cannot be doubted that they who daily and accurately survey themselves and their own hearts, though they may indeed escape many of those evils which the generality of mankind, who live as it were by chance, fall into, yet, in consequence of that very care and study, see so much the more clearly their own impurity, and contract a greater abhorrence of themselves and a more reverential dread of the Divine judgments. And it is certain that the holier any one is, the viler will he be in his own eyes; and I may also add, the viler he is in his own eyes, the more dear, precious, and honorable will he be in the sight of God. Oh, my brethren! be entreated to study your own hearts better. Be less abroad in things that concern you not. There is work enough within you; heaps of base lusts, and self-deceits, and follies, that you see not yet; and many advantages of good things you seem to see in yourselves, that indeed are not there. Self-love is a flattering glass, which represents us to ourselves much fairer than we are; therefore turn from it, if you desire a true account of yourselves, and look into the pure and faithful mirror of God's Law. Oh! what deformities will that discover, which you never saw nor thought of before; it will make you the lowest of all persons in your own eyes."

Now it is not an agreeable dilemma, but we are compelled to choose between Leighton's views of sanctification, and those of the Higher Life school. With him, and with all for whom he spoke, every renewed heart is the seat of active lusts which keep on warring against the soul until death ends the contest. With them, one who has obtained "the blessing," is discharged from this conflict, serves God perfectly, does not sin, and has no occasion to ask for daily forgiveness. Nor is this the only characteristic difference. In vain will the writings of Leighton, Flavel, Halyburton, Baxter, and their compeers, be searched for any evidence of a desire to magnify their own individual experience. There are times and occasions when a Christian may properly say to his friends, "Come and hear, all ye that fear God, and I will declare what He hath done for my soul." But such occasions will not come every day and in all companies. It certainly produces an unpleasant impression, to hear a person *habitually* relating his own experience. These writers can hardly be aware how much they talk about themselves. To be frank, there is so much of it that it puts rather a sharp strain upon the reader's forbearance. It would materially reduce the bulk of their publications, to cancel one-half of the matter that is strictly personal to themselves. The reason they offer for giving it this prominence, is, that they design hereby to exalt the grace of God, and to help others on in the way they have trod. No doubt this was the motive. But the end does not always justify the means. The common conception of true religion, is, that it abases a sinner in his own eyes: that it cures him in a measure (unfortunately, in a measure only) of wishing to attract attention to himself: and above all, that it makes him very modest in describing such of his own exercises as may seem to breathe of extraordinary communications of Divine grace.

It were uncharitable to say that this rule is violated in the books before us, from any spirit of ostentation. Certainly there is no *consciousness* of any such spirit. But when every topic touched upon by them, is illustrated or enforced by citations from their own experience, and the lesson addressed to others, is, practically, that all persons must be led in the same way: "You ought to do thus and so, just as I did:" "You can do this, for I did it:" "I obtained instant sanctification, and so can you:" "I am filled with light and love unspeakable, and so may you be:"—even a kindly disposed reader can with difficulty repress the feeling, that the *Ego* is too prominent, especially for a system in which self is supposed to be nothing, and God everything; for, as Wilberforce justly said, "it is the peculiarity of the Christian religion, that humility and holiness increase in equal proportions."* Nor this alone. The suspicion *will* arise, that fewer leaves would have been taken from their private Diaries, if there had not been a dearth of examples from other

---

* Some six or seven years after Mr. Simeon's ordination, a faithful friend wrote to him, warning him against vanity. He frankly acknowledged the infirmity; thanked his friend for the admonition; and, added—"It would be easier to erase that great letter 'I' from all the books in the kingdom, than to hide it for one hour from the eyes of a vain person."

sources. It speaks ill for the system, very ill, that its advocates should have to pass by, almost entirely, the generous stores of evangelical Biography within the reach of every intelligent Christian, and confine themselves so much to their own personal history, and their interviews with those around them. It suggests the apprehension that the type of religion which they affect, is not quite coincident with that which has given life and joy and power, to the great champions of the faith, in the successive ages of the Church.

If these things are so, it follows, that the scheme we are considering, is too superficial and unstable to yield that solid and durable comfort, which is the yearning of every renewed soul. Its teachers may plead their own experience as precluding this conclusion : but to make the plea available, it must be proved to the satisfaction of others, that there is any really firm foundation for the exalted happiness they profess to enjoy. There are those who find in the "wilderness-life," a freedom and joy which they would be slow to exchange for the rapture of an imaginary unsinning estate.

To pursue this topic a step farther, how can that sort of peace be coveted, which is held by so fragile a tenure? The doctrine is, that you lose "the blessing," *i. e.*, you fall from your condition of "practical holiness" and full assurance, the moment you cease to exercise that unquestioning faith which commenced with your "consecration;" and a single sin is at once effect and proof that your faith *has* given way. That it is a common occurrence for believers to lose the blessing, is, as we have seen, freely admitted. How could it be otherwise? If, like "ordinary Christians," they are accustomed to "examine themselves," and especially by the standard of perfect holiness, it is no marvel they should often fear that they may have sinned. "Have I done nothing amiss during the past week? Have I omitted nothing which I might have done for the honor of my Lord? Have I uttered no unkind, no rash, no idle word? Have I withheld no word which might have been helpful to some fellow-creature? Have I wasted no time? Have I indulged no untoward appetite or temper—no pride, no envy, no thought of my being better than others, no selfishness in any form? Has it been my successful aim to seek God's glory in my eating and drinking, my talking and walking, my writing and reading? Have all my thoughts been heavenward? Has love to God inflamed my heart every moment, and fired my zeal? Can I say with a

good conscience that I have been fully up to the requirements of that law which reaches to my very motives and emotions, even so that, as I honestly believe, God's book of remembrance contains, for the last week, no charge opposite my name, of anything which He has given me the means of knowing to be sinful?" Some such self-inquest as this will (certainly should) be now and then gone through by every denizen of the "Higher Life" realm: and the issue cannot be problematical. Those who stand the test, must be the few: the favored many—"favored," because blessed with more light—must inevitably fail. This is virtually conceded: "I am sure *many* a heart is going bowed down in secret from this fatal habit of doubting. *Many* of my readers could, I am convinced, testify to the truth of this. They know that their wavering faith is the cause of their wavering experience. One day they have believed that Jesus did indeed save them from sin and from sinning, and it has been so in their experience. But the next day they have looked at themselves, and have begun to doubt, and their experience has corresponded to their doubts." *
And if this be so very common a case, what makes this style of life a Canaan, and that of

* *Walking in the Light.*

other Christians, the desert? Would it have been a comfortable allotment to the Hebrews, had they spent their forty years in perpetually crossing and recrossing the Jordan—one day or one week in the land of promise, and the next, back again among the Amalekites and Moabites? The blessing of which God's word speaks, is not quite so easily lost: for "who shall separate us?"

The directions for recovering the Higher Life blessing, reveal anew that fatal mistake as to the nature of faith which vitiates the entire scheme: "Believe steadfastly through everything, no matter what comes, just what you believed at first upon your entering into this blessed 'Higher Life;' and never doubt it again. If the step of faith you took then, was, to reckon yourself to be dead indeed unto sin, continue thus to reckon without wavering. If it was to believe that the blood of Jesus cleansed you from all unrighteousness, go on believing this steadily, and without any compromise. Or if it simply came to you as a faith that Jesus saved you fully, exercise that very same faith now, and keep exercising it continually without intermission." (1) Here is a thrice-repeated statement, that true faith consists not in believing on the Lord Jesus Christ, but in believing that we are renewed and fully sanctified. There is no such definition of faith in the word of God. (2) We have the assumption already noted and exposed, that we can believe by putting forth a volition to believe; without so much as a hint that prayer is the true resource for a doubting soul. With a simplicity that would be amusing, in any other relation, the solitary injunction is reiterated : " To regain your perfect sanctification, believe, as you believed at first, that you already have it !" What Martin Luther would have thought of this novel kind of faith, can easily be conjectured. What he would have said, in reply to such counsel, is matter of record. " Faith is no such easy matter as our opposers imagine when they say: ' Believe; Believe; how *easy* is it to believe :' [One might suspect that the Reformer, by some sort of second-sight, had read these books three centuries before they appeared : or is it so, that no error of our day, is new?] Neither is it a mere human work which I can perform for myself: but is a Divine power in the heart by which we are new born, and whereby we are able to overcome the mighty power of the devil and of death,—as Paul says to the Colossians, ' In whom ye are raised up again through the faith which God works. '" (3) The Christian who has lost "the blessing," would naturally infer that he had fallen into sin, and wish to find out wherein his fault lay. And just here, conflicting counsels might embarrass him. "Let nothing shake your faith [*i. e.* faith in your good estate]. Should even sin unhappily overtake you, still you must not doubt. 'If we confess our sins, He is faithful and just to forgive us our sins, and to cleanse us from *all* unrighteousness.' Confess your sin, therefore, immediately upon the discovery of it, and believe at once that God *does* forgive it, and *does* again cleanse you from *all* unrighteousness; and go on believing it." But how is he to discover his sin without looking within, and comparing himself with the lessons of the unerring word? Yet in the same chapter he is told: "Satan has been turning your attention to yourself. He says to you, 'Look at your heart and your life. See how cold you are, how indifferent, how far from being what you ought to be. How can you for a moment dare to believe that Jesus saves *you* and makes you holy?' And you have listened to him, and turning your eyes off of Jesus, have begun to doubt." What warrant has the writer for ascribing this self-inspection to Satan? Does the Holy Spirit never suggest reflections of this kind to a Christian? Have they not, ten thousand times over, been but too well founded? Is Satan more likely than the Spirit of God, to disturb the complacency of a self-deceived professor? Were it not as well to say to one, in the circumstances supposed: "Examine thyself, whether thou art in the faith:" and then offer the prayer, "Create in me a clean heart, O God, and renew a right spirit within me"?

(4) How perplexing must it be for a person, attempting to follow these counsels, to know whether he has succeeded or not! "I am admonished (he might say) that I can regain 'the blessing' only by exercising the same faith in my being dead to sin and wholly sanctified, which I had at my consecration. I try to do this. I try to believe that it is all well with me. I do my best to believe that I have gone up to the plane of the Higher Life, and am again living without sin. But I am not so sure of this, as I would like to be. Far down in my breast, there are latent misgivings which I dare neither suppress nor express. What *can* I do?" Have not voices like these been often heard? And what is done to relieve such disciples, by saying to them: "Believe, Believe, that it is well with you, and it *is* well"? How would it answer to say to the faltering soul: "You *need* not mistake your condition. God is

the Hearer of prayer, and He can re-assure your hope. Suppose you look up to Him, in the name of our blessed Mediator, and cry: 'Search me, O God, and know my heart: try me, and know my thoughts: and see if there be any wicked way in me, and lead me in the way everlasting.'" Would not this counsel be as intelligible, as Scriptural, and as likely to conduct to true peace of mind, as that with which it is contrasted?

(5) The duty and importance of self-examination, will be generally acknowledged. At the opposite extreme of the scale, is the morbid habit of constantly scrutinizing one's exercises. It is a capital objection to the system under review, that teaching the Christian to regard his "consecration" as the grand object of his attainment, and his holiness and comfort as depending upon his not faltering in the exercise of his consecrating faith; it necessarily tends to keep him much engrossed with the question, "Is my faith genuine? Am I really taking Christ for my sanctification? Am I in no danger of allowing my faith so to decline as to lose 'the blessing?'" Alike in preserving and in recovering his perfect holiness, his attention must be directed to the one vital point of his own faith. It is true, they caution the believer against consulting his own frames, and exhort him to look

out of himself to Christ. But when told, scores of times, that everything depends upon his maintaining in vigorous exercise, not a simple trust in the Saviour, but the faith with which he believed himself to be wholly sanctified, what can restrain him from the habitual study of his faith? And why, if this be the true idea of faith, should he be restrained, if that were possible? Say, then, whether a scheme can be favorable to serenity of mind and joy in God, which thus hangs the believer's happiness entirely upon his own conscious faith in his own faith—an abnormal faith which is clothed with an autocratic sovereignty over the intellect and the affections, and is yet liable to constant failure! Upon no such contingent and fluctuating base as this, do their assurance and comfort repose, who are still threading the "wilderness." God has provided some better thing for them. They have 1st the everlasting covenant of grace, wherein the Father gave His Son the people who were to be ransomed by His blood. Jer. 32 : 40; John 17 : 2–6. 2dly. The vital union between Christ and His members, in virtue of which, because He lives, they shall live also. John 15 : 1–5; 14 : 19. 3dly. The atoning death and resurrection of Christ. Rom. 5 : 8–10. 4th. The pledged omnipotence of God, that they shall never perish. John 10 : 27–30; 1 Cor. 1 : 8; 1 Pet. 1 : 5; Phil. 1 : 6. 5th. The Holy Spirit keeping alive, and enabling them to discern in themselves, faith and love and all those graces to which the promises of life are made. 1 Cor. 2 : 12; 1 John 4 : 13–16; 3 : 14, 18, 19, 21, 24. 6th. The inward witness of the Spirit, witnessing with their spirits that they are the children of God. Rom. 8 : 16. Such is the foundation, more solid and durable than the granite mountains, which the infinite love and wisdom of God have provided for the security and comfort of His children. It is offered alike to them all. Is it not amazing that any among them should decline this tender, and choose, rather, to entrust their peace and strength to a conscious belief in their own faith? What wonder if, a few years hence, the historian shall have to repeat Mr. Wesley's chronicle concerning the Perfectionists of his day: "Among his converts, at first a few and afterwards scores and hundreds, claimed to have reached perfection at once. Although, as he says, he never had an experience like theirs, and to the last never professed to have attained it, still he was favorably impressed with their earnestness, and not disposed to question their sincerity. But he soon saw that they began to lose what they called their 'perfection.' Even Miss Bosanquet, so often mentioned, was one of this number. And in 1770 he confesses that *not one in thirty retained it*. 'Many hundreds in London,' he says, ' were made partakers of it within sixteen or eighteen months; but I doubt whether *twenty* of them are now as holy and happy as they were.'" What is there in the Higher Life scheme of perfection, to save it from a kindred destiny? "Every plant which my Heavenly Father hath not planted, shall be rooted up."—We are shut up, then, to the conclusion, that this system is radically deficient in respect to the provision it makes for the abiding comfort and habitual assurance of believers.

CHAPTER XV.

HIGHER LIFE EXAMPLES.

The question will naturally be asked, what estimate is to be put upon the numerous *examples* cited by these writers in illustration of their views? Those who are familiar with their books will have observed, what indeed has already been mentioned, that they seldom enter the familiar and fertile field of Christian Biography, and when they do, it is not with much success. The author of the "*Higher Christian Life*" dilates upon the experience of Luther and Merle d'Aubigné. If it be designed to produce them as witnesses in behalf of his theory of sanctification, this is a very unwarrantable use of their names. (V. chap. I. above.) Their writings show that it was a widely different idea of sanctification which they found in the Scriptures. What really happened with these two eminent men, and with various other persons who are placed on the witness-stand, was just what happens frequently before our own eyes. After being partially enlightened and entering upon the service of God, Christian men, ever and anon, receive further illumination from the Divine Spirit, are inspired with fresh faith and love and zeal, and give themselves with new ardor and devotedness to the cause of Christ. This is not so rare a phenomenon that it need be dignified with the ambiguous name of a "second conversion;" nor is it quite apparent why examples of the kind should be adduced as if they were illustrative of what is peculiar in the Higher Life scheme. If they are to claim as sponsor every Christian who exchanges a life of sloth and formality, or of zeal without knowledge, for a life of fervent love and intelligent activity in his Master's service, their witnesses will rise up, an exceeding great army. But a very large proportion of these conscripts would be surprised to find themselves enrolled as exemplars of a perfect sanctification. Even the cases described in detail, as occurring under the immediate counsel of the Higher Life teachers, would carry, to an impartial mind, no conviction of the trustworthiness of the theory. One thing is certain: there is nothing in the Bible akin to the more prominent scenes, which are described in these narratives. We read of the agitation and alarm of the three thousand at Pentecost, of Simon Magus, and of the jailer of Philippi, when their eyes were opened to their sin and ruin. We see this repeated daily with awakened sinners. But where is there a solitary instance, from Genesis to Revelation, of a *believer* passing through a prolonged struggle, weeping, agonizing, crying out, his whole frame so convulsed and exhausted that he has to be carried well-nigh lifeless to his bed—and all that he may obtain, not a good hope, through grace, for this he has already, but *perfect holiness?* Could any serious reader of the Scriptures, unbiased by a theory, discover the faintest hint of a process like this in the counsels they give for growing in grace and becoming assimilated to God? Allowing that in a few specific instances, violent convulsions of this nature may have issued in the attainment of peace and a holy life, who that has noted the effects of solemn religious truth pressed home upon a susceptible nature, and reinforced by the sympathies of excited bystanders, would think of holding up such experiences as models for Christians generally? Nor this alone. In the great majority of the cases enumerated, the testing element of time is fatally wanting. We are told that A, B, and C, on performing the act of consecration, emerged from the doubt and darkness of the lower, into the light and joy of the Higher,

Christian life. How long they kept their high estate, except in a few instances, is not mentioned. If, as we have endeavored to show, the prescribed process is one which peculiarly invites to self-deception, it would be no strange thing should there be occasion in the course of two or three years, to repeat Mr. Wesley's melancholy testimony, "not one in thirty retained the blessing."

These remarks may serve to show how much weight is to be attached to the personal narratives embraced in these books. And it is proper to accompany them with a renewed protest against the liberal use of examples, as tributary to the system, which really have no affinity with it as a distinct theory of sanctification. Narratives of this kind, albeit written in good faith, if not carefully analyzed and weighed, may pass for much more than they are worth, as vouchers of some favorite speculation. Even should they seem, on a fair examination, to bear the interpretation put upon them, it still remains to test the speculation by the only infallible standard It is not enough for you to say, " I *know* this doctrine is true, for I have *experienced* it all." Experience is not a test of truth—until it has itself been proved by the word of God. The whole history of fanaticism illustrates the soundness of this principle. When a person comes to us detailing some very novel experience, or claiming to have been made the depository of some special revelation, the proper response is, "What is written in the law? How readest thou?" "To the law and to the testimony; if they speak not according to this word, it is because there is no light in them." In this way, remembering that "many false prophets are gone out into the world," we are "to try the spirits, whether they are of God." That an experience may be very peculiar and yet Scriptural, cannot be doubted. We may not limit the Holy Spirit in shaping and guiding the inner life of His children. Even if one profess to have attained perfect holiness, and that in a way unknown to the Church, while we bring the assumption to the statute-book and prove it a phantasm, we may find much in the Christian character of the party concerned, that is worthy of our love and imitation.

It were a delicate matter to discuss the accounts given by some of these writers of *their own* exercises. Not that they would shrink from it; for they expatiate on the subject in a manner not only to challenge for their experience the closest scrutiny —but to show that, in their judgment, it would be a great loss to their readers should they fail to

study it. But what is the real value of this type of experience as to other persons? The substance of it is, that they are raised above the world, are free from sin, indifferent to sorrow, and enjoy a beatific life. "In reckoning myself dead, I found that I *was* practically dead unto sin. I found that the old man was actually put off, and the other actually put on. I was enabled in short to walk in the Spirit, and therefore not to fulfil the lusts of the flesh. . . . All the past of my Christian course seems comparatively wasted. I was a child of God it is true; but my growth was stinted, and my stature feeble. Now I have begun to grow. Now there are no limits to the possibilities of my future. I have entered upon the way of holiness; and my path, even mine, will be, I humbly believe, as the path of the just, shining more and more unto the perfect day." *
"I feel led to say, that I find my peace to flow as a river, with rare cross-currents or return tides. As from day to day I feel this increasing power of God raise me above the snares and sorrows of life, the Christ formed within and giving dominion over the world, the heavenly and continuous joy that fills my soul, the presence of Jesus to my consciousness in all my life, I find myself invol-

* H. W. S.

untarily exclaiming, again and again, 'This is *salvation*—a salvation worthy of its Author.' Those around me seem hardly so visibly present as does the person of my Lord. My heart is as a string upon which the wind of the Spirit blows softly, even through life's busiest scenes, and at times, when alone, the melody seems more almost than my frame can bear. I have understood as I have sat at eventide alone among the trees, how the father of the faithful felt when the three came to him, and with the rustling branches have sat in a thrill of momentary expectation of a presence that seemed almost ready to manifest itself to sense. Although the small vessel is full to its present capacity, I know that it can be enlarged; for of the increase of His government and peace within His kingdom, 'there shall be no end.' And yet it is but moment by moment, and by a continuing faith—which, like breathing, has become a holy habit—that I can thus live. I tremble as I see the dangers on every hand, and the many who, for want of watching and prayer, have fallen from the steadfastness of their faith." *

This state of ecstasy has been reached by many persons before the time of "H. W. S." and "R.

---

* *Through Death to Life*, R. P. S.

P. S." It is recorded of Gregory Lopez, that, "having for the space of three years continued that ejaculation, 'Thy will be done in time and in eternity,' repeating it as often as he breathed, God Almighty discovered to him that infinite treasure of the pure and continued act of faith and love, with silence and resignation: so that he came to say that during the thirty-six years he lived afterward, he always continued in his inward man that pure act of love, without ever uttering the least petition, ejaculation, or anything that was sensible or sprung from nature."

We may not question that there are sometimes gentle illapses of the Divine Spirit into the devout soul, which do for a while, detach it, as it were, from earth and sense, and bring it into sweet communion with God. The prevalent feeling with those who have thus gone up on the mount and seen the glory of God, has been that so exalted a favor was something too sacred to be habitually talked about. One thing is certain. The thought which largely absorbs the writers we have quoted—which they dilate upon—which they hold up as one of the blissful results of their "consecration," and an end which all Christians should aim at—is, the thought of *their own immeasurable happiness.* This is the issue of their perfect sanctification, and the want of it, the sad privation incident to every lower stage of the Christian life. Now there is a savor of *selfishness* about this experience, which must make "ordinary Christians" distrustful of it. The New Testament no where sets forth a present, unalloyed happiness, as one of the great ends at which we are to aim. It has linked together duty and happiness. It portrays a life of godliness, as the only life attended with true enjoyment. But it assuredly does not depict perfect felicity in this world—still less a solitary, quiescent felicity—as one of the main objects to which the believer is to aspire, and one of the controlling motives which is to animate his obedience. The reason clearly is, that it is of the essence of genuine religion to divert the thoughts from one's self, and send them both God-ward and man-ward—upward in grateful, adoring love toward the Father of all, and outward in benevolent sympathies toward one's fellow-creatures. Instead of saying, "How perfectly happy I am! I can think only of the blessedness of my lot;" the feeling is, "What can I do to bring others to Christ, and make them sharers of the peace and joy to be found in Him alone?" A generous concern for others may co-exist with the rapture described by our authors. But the whole tendency of their instructions and experiences, is, to make this rapture an *end;* and hence, notwithstanding disavowals, to foster a religion of frames and feelings.* If this were not the case, the inheritors of this peerless treasure would be pre-eminent in their exertions for the well-being of others. Rejoicing in the exercise of an imperial faith, released from sin, walking heavenward under the full beams of the Sun of Righteousness, they should excel less favored believers as much in loveliness of character, and in their active labors for the salvation of sinners and the spread of the Gospel, as they do in their greater light and purity and happiness. No one will charge that they are indifferent to these vital interests,—albeit a continuous ecstasy like that of Gregory Lopez must needs turn any life into a nullity. But it does not appear that the disciples of this school, excellent as they are, are *conspicuously* better than many who are still beset

"With sins and doubts and fears:"

---

* Even Dr. Payson, at one stage of his religious progress, "was so anxious for happy frames, that, unconsciously, he made the obtaining of such frames, the immediate *end* of his offices of devotion,—and graduated his hope according to his success therein."

—that they are more humble, more gentle, more affectionate, more cheerful; that they surpass them in labors and sacrifices for the instruction of the ignorant, the recovery of the perishing, the relief of the suffering; that they carry a brighter presence into the varied scenes of social life; or clothe religion in a more winning garb to the eyes of unbelievers. As they claim to stand upon so much higher ground that they look down with sympathy upon their brethren "in the wilderness," we have a right to say to them, "What do ye more than others? We do not question the full tide of holy joy which, you say, is flowing through your breasts, but how much is the world the better for it? Wherein do you exemplify more beautifully the graces of the Spirit, or labor for Christ more assiduously and successfully than those who, day by day, go lovingly about their work, less heedful of their own frames than of the welfare of others, and careful only to be found doing the Master's will?" In so far as human agencies are concerned, the greatest moral power that could have place in our world, would be a *sinless man*. In the very fact of asserting their freedom from sin, these persons (ascribing their elevation of course to Divine grace) claim to be more Christ-like than any other Christians. It would be absurd to suppose that such a state of things could exist, without authenticating itself to other eyes than their own—nay, to other eyes much more than to their own. When a person said to Mr. Newton, "The great saints in the Calendar were many of them great sinners," he replied, "They were poor saints indeed, if they did not feel themselves to be great sinners." We do not at all impeach the standing of these teachers as sincere believers: but we must insist, that if they are arrayed in that holiness which they vaunt, the most superfluous office they could assume, and the most improbable they would assume, would be that of proclaiming it to the world. As well might the sun on the meridian announce in audible utterance, that he was in the heavens. Such holiness could not help being known. True Christians, certainly, of every name, would recognize the heavenly lineaments, and pay it their glad homage. But if in the midst of their benedictions, the bright impersonation should begin to *expatiate on its own perfection,* what then? Would not the image of gold turn to clay before their eyes? And might they not, perchance, turn away from the shrine one, by one, silent and sad?

Let us hear on this topic, the eloquent words

of one * whom nature, education, and grace, conspired to adorn with their richest gifts; and whose sun, in the inscrutable providence of God, went down while it was yet day :

"The belief in Christian perfectibility seems inapplicable to individual practice from the very nature of Christian holiness. *Were a perfect man to exist, he himself would be the last to know it ;* † for the highest stage of advancement is the lowest descent in *humility*. As long as this humility is necessary to the fulness of the Christian character, it would seem that it is of the essence of the constant growth in grace (however encouraged by holy joy and and inward testimonies) to see itself lowlier as God exalts it higher. It is as one who stands by the margin of a lake, and gazes on his own image close beneath him :—conceive this contemplator of himself borne gradually aloft toward the heavens, and the image which he still beholds as he soars, will deepen in proportion as he rises! Besides this operation of humility, it must be remembered that the spiritual life, if it be a pro-

---

* William Archer Butler, of the University of Dublin.

† It is surely significant that this identical remark should be made by so many of the eminent men quoted in this book—as it is by very many elsewhere. There is a great mistake lying *somewhere*, between them and the Higher Life school.

gressive life, involves a progressively increasing knowledge of God. Now, although the spirit of man assuredly must brighten in purity, as thus in faith and love it approaches the great source of all holiness, it must also appreciate far more accurately the force of the *contrast* between itself and its mighty model; nay, its very adoration, apprehending, as all affection does, more profoundly the excellencies of its object, must impress upon it its own comparative nothingness: and thus, as it becomes relatively more perfect, it may be said to feel itself absolutely less so. In truth, it is only piety, and piety fervent and exalted, that can really feel how immeasurably far it is from perfect holiness. There are distances so great, that all calculation of distance is neglected or impossible. We cannot tell how far is the nearest fixed star, and we know that the mass of mankind would conjecture it a few miles at most: could we approach *nearer*, we should, for the first time, learn *how far* we were! Surely it is so with our religious estimates of approximation to the light and glory of God: the earth-born crowd afar, if they think at all of the matter, never dream themselves so darkly, so remotely exiled; it is only he who struggles nearer, and much nearer, that begins at length to perceive the true amount of the distance. And thus, whatever be the doctrine of Christian perfectibility collected out of this Epistle of St. John, it certainly can have little relation to the earthly saint's estimate of *his own* piety: his ejaculation will still be with David,—'I will run the way of Thy commandments, *when Thou shalt enlarge* my heart;' 'My soul cleaveth unto the dust; *quicken Thou me* according to Thy word:'—his highest offerings, as he contemplates those exceeding broad commandments that involve the whole sacrifice of the man to God, still appearing to himself all unworthy of the altar on which they are laid. He will scarcely dare to say, with the Holy One of God, 'I have *finished* the work which Thou gavest me to do' (John 17 : 4). Nay, I doubt not but it is the very genius of that divine *love* which is the bond of perfectness, to be lovingly dissatisfied with its own inadequacy; and such a worshipper in his best hours will feel that though 'love' be indeed, as these divines so earnestly insist, 'the *fulfilling* of the Law,' his love is itself imperfect, deficient in degree, and deficient in constancy; and that in this life it can, at best, be only the germ of that charity which, 'never failing,' is to form the moving principle of the life of eternity. And though he shed tears of humble gratitude to think that his Heavenly Master is pleased to accept such love as this, and even to call it, in a modified sense, a fulfilment of His Gospel-Law, it does not appear that the believer's *consciousness of this fulfilment* (were it ever so absolute and conclusive) could itself form a practical motive of much importance in the Christian life. Let him be but assured, that the aspirations of his heart and the labors of his hand are a duty, and acceptable to God, and I cannot conceive that his aspirations will be less ardent or his labors less efficient, though he should hesitate to believe himself arrived at the fulness of evangelical perfection, and though he should still continue to appropriate the warning words of the text,—'If I say that I have *no sin*, I deceive myself;' and still joyfully reiterate the blessed sequel,—'but if I confess, He is faithful and just to forgive!'"

The profound philosophy of the foregoing argument, even more than its faultless rhetoric, may well commend it, not to the mere reading, but to the careful study, of those who have deluded themselves into the belief, that a self-conscious perfection is the fruit and evidence of great nearness to God. "Not he that commendeth himself is approved, but whom the LORD commendeth."

CHAPTER XVI.

TRUSTWORTHY EXPERIENCES—CONCLUSION.

As we have been so often invited by the Higher Life writers to contemplate examples of perfectly sanctified believers, it would not be proper to close this discussion without giving a few leaves from the private history of Christians who had not obtained "the blessing." A very cloud of witnesses stand within call. Their names irradiate the annals of the Church all adown the ages. It must suffice to summon four or five. We pass abruptly on meeting them into a different atmosphere from that we have been breathing; for here we encounter the element of *penitential* love. The absence of it is one of the most marked characteristics of the adverse type of experience. These faithful "servants of the Most High God" knew nothing of a piety without penitence. Their religion was not that of the seventh of Romans, nor of the eighth of Romans, exclusively; but of both combined. They were humbled in the consciousness of a daily inward conflict, calling for daily forgivness; but their "assurance" was as complete as that of "the ninety and nine who need no repentance." Let us hear them.

JOHN OWEN: 1616–1683. By his Puritan brethren, he was called the "Prince of Divines." His works are comprised in twenty-one large octavo volumes. Those who are conversant with his exhaustive Treatises on Psalm 130, on the *Holy Spirit*, on *Temptation*, on the *Mortification of Sin in Believers*, and on *Spiritual Mindedness*, will agree, that on questions pertaining to experimental and casuistical piety, there is no higher uninspired authority extant. His Essay on the *Dominion of Sin and Grace*, is founded on Romans 6 : 14: "For sin shall not have dominion over you; for ye are not under the law, but under grace." A brief extract follows:

"The conflict with sin, making continual repentance and mortification absolutely necessary, will continue with us whilst we are in this world. Pretences of perfection here are contrary to the Scriptures, contrary to the universal experience of all believers, and contrary to the sense and conscience of them by whom they are pleaded, as they make it evident every day. We pray against it, strive against it, groan for deliverance from it

—and that, by the grace of Christ healing our nature, not without success. Howbeit this success extends not unto its absolute abolition whilst we are in this world. It will abide in us until the union of the soul and body, wherein it hath incorporated itself, be dissolved. This is our lot and portion: this is the consequent of our apostasy from God, and the depravation of our nature thereby." "What advantage then have we from the Gospel?" Owen answers: "(1) The continuance of sin is the ground, reason and occasion of the exercise of all grace, and putting a lustre on our obedience." He instances repentance, humility, resignation to the Divine will, loving and longing for the enjoyment of Christ, etc. "(2) Christ pledges such supplies of grace as shall prevent sin from regaining its *dominion* over the soul. (3) There is pardoning mercy for the believer, which disarms sin of its *condemning* power. (4) At death sin shall be utterly abolished."

The truth of this, in both its parts, was attested in Owen's own experience. Only a month or two before his death he wrote to a friend: "I find you and I are much in complaining. For my part I must say, And is there not a cause? So much deadness, so much inspirituality, so much weakness in faith, coldness in love, instability in holy meditations, as I find in myself, is cause sufficient of complaints. But is there not cause also of thanksgiving and joy in the Lord? Are there not reasons for them? When I begin to think of them, I am overwhelmed. They are great. They are glorious. They are inexpressible. Shall I now invite you to this great duty of rejoicing more in God?"

John Bunyan: 1628–1688. It has been pointed out in a former chapter, that if Bunyan had taken up with "Perfectionism," of whatever type, the "*Pilgrim's Progress*" would never have been written. Not one sentence of that immortal Allegory lends the least countenance to the Higher Life speculation. And as to the author's account of his own heart, here it is—written in the ripeness of his Christian experience: "I find this day seven abominations in my heart: (1) Inclining to unbelief. (2) Suddenly to forget the love and mercy that Christ manifesteth. (3) A leaning to the works of the law. (4) Wanderings and coldness in prayer. (5) To forget to watch for that I pray for. (6) Apt to murmur because I have no more, and yet ready to abuse what I have. (7) I can do none of those things which God commands me, but my corruptions will thrust in themselves. *When I would do good, evil is present with me.*

"These things I continually see and feel, and am afflicted and oppressed with: yet the wisdom of God doth order them for my good: (1) They make me abhor myself. (2) They keep me from trusting my heart. (3) They convince me of the insufficiency of all inherent righteousness. (4) They show me the necessity of flying to Jesus. (5) They press me to pray unto God. (6) They show me the need I have to watch and be sober. (7) And provoke me to pray unto God, through Christ, to help me, and carry me through this world."

John Newton: 1725–1807. The Higher Life writers hold in great disparagement the experience which involves a conflict with indwelling sin. Here is Newton's selection from the whole Bible, of a text which describes the the true believer: "Were I to define a Christian, or rather to describe him at large, I know no text I would choose sooner, as a ground for the subject, than Gal. 5 : 17: 'For the flesh lusteth against the spirit, and the spirit against the flesh: and these are contrary the one to the other, so that ye cannot do the things that ye would.' A Christian has noble aims which distinguish him from the rest of mankind. His leading principles, motives, and desires are all supernatural and divine. Could he do as he would, there is not a spirit before the throne should excel him in holiness, love, and obedience. He would tread in the very footsteps of his Saviour, fill up every moment in His service, and employ every breath in His praise. This he would do, but alas! he cannot. Against this desire of the spirit, there is a contrary desire and working of a corrupt nature, which meets him at every turn. He has a beautiful copy set before him: he is enamored with it; and though he does not expect to equal it, he writes carefully after it, and longs to attain to the nearest possible imitation. But indwelling sin and Satan continually jog his hand and spoil his strokes. You cannot, madam, form a right judgment of yourself, except you make due allowance for those things which are not peculiar to yourself, but common to all who have spiritual perception, and are indeed the inseparable appendages of this mortal state. If it were not so, why should the most spiritual and gracious people be so ready to confess themselves vile and worthless? One eminent branch of our holiness, is a sense of shame and humiliation for those evils which

are known only to ourselves, and to Him who
searches our hearts, joined with an acquiescence
in Jesus, who is appointed of God, wisdom, righteousness, sanctification, and redemption. I will
venture to assure you, that though you will possess a more stable peace, in proportion as the
Lord enables you to live more simply upon the
blood, righteousness, and grace of the Mediator,
you will never grow into a better opinion of
yourself than you have at present. The nearer
you are brought to Him, the quicker sense you
will have of your continual need of Him, and
thereby your admiration of His power, love,
and compassion, will increase likewise from year
to year."

Elsewhere Newton says: "I know not that I
have had a doubt of a quarter of an hour's continuance, with respect to my acceptance in the
Beloved, for many years past. But oh, the
multiplied instances of stupidity, ingratitude,
impatience and rebellion, to which my conscience has been witness! And as every heart
knows its own bitterness, I have generally heard
the same complaints from others of the Lord's
people with whom I have conversed, even from
those who have appeared to be eminently gracious and spiritual. . . . We are prone to spir-

itual pride, to self-dependence, to vain confidence, to creature attachments, and to a train of evils." *

Archibald Alexander, D. D.: 1772–1851. This is a household name in some thousands of American homes. At the head, for forty years, of a large Theological Seminary, its numerous Alumni regarded him through life, as the highest authority of this century on matters of experimental religion. His son and biographer, a man of kindred spirit and of brilliant endowments, says of him: "While he was burdened [habitually] with a sense of *indwelling sin*, he was eminently free from doubts as to his own acceptance with God. Though he never said so, we are persuaded that his habitual state of mind was one of *confirmed assurance*." . . . "There is reason to believe, that during most of his life he suffered from inward struggles and temptations. Yet again and again did he come forth from his study, radiant with spiritual refreshment. His religion was characteristically composing and tranquil. As he advanced in years he became more and more happy; until at the very close he was happiest of all."

Some years before his death, Dr. Alexander

---

* Works, 8vo, pp. 213, 60.

composed a devotional exercise, doubtless with reference to his own case, a few sentences from which will show what a stranger he was to the Higher Life scheme of sanctification: "I am deeply convinced, that my best duties have fallen far short of the perfection of Thy law, and have been so mingled with sin in the performance, that I might justly be condemned for the most fervent prayer I ever made. And I would confess with shame and contrition, that I am not only chargeable with sin in the act, but that there is a law of my members warring against the law of my mind, aiming to bring me into captivity to the law of sin and death. This corrupt nature is the source of innumerable evil thoughts and desires, damps the exercise of faith and love, and stands in the way of well-doing, so that when I would do good, evil is present with me. And so deep and powerful is this remaining depravity, that all efforts to eradicate or subdue it, are vain without the aid of Divine grace. And when at any time I obtain a glimpse of the depth and turpitude of the sin of my nature, I am overwhelmed, and constrained to exclaim with Job, 'I abhor myself and repent in dust and ashes.'" *

Then follows a plea for mercy through the

* *Life*, p. 615.

Mediation of the adorable Redeemer, with various other petitions suited to the case of an aged pilgrim near the end of his journey,—altogether a very remarkable and affecting prayer, the very reading of which must be a means of grace to any serious-minded person.

Robert Murray McCheyne: 1813–1843. A name full of fragrance. A sentence or two must suffice to show the tone of his interior life—a life overflowing with love to God, and *therefore* keenly alive to the stains of sin: "Affliction will certainly purify a believer. How boldly he says it, 'I shall come out like gold'! Ah, how much dross there is in every one of you, dear believers, and in your pastor! 'When I would do good, evil is present with me.' Oh that all the dross may be left behind in the furnace!"—"I think I was never brought to see the wickedness of my heart as I do now. Yet do I not feel it as many sweet Christians do, while they are high above it, and seem to look down into a depth of iniquity, deep, deep in their bosoms. Now it appears to me as if my feet were actually in the miry clay, and I only wonder that I am kept from open sin."— "Oh what a cursed body of sin we bear, that we should be obliged by it to break these sweet Gospel-rules! How much more useful might we be, if we were only more free from pride, self-conceit, personal vanity, or some secret sin that our heart knows! Oh, hateful sins, that destroy our peace, and ruin souls! Oh, to have Brainerd's heart for perfect holiness! to be holy as God is holy; pure as Christ is pure; perfect as our Father in heaven is perfect!"

WILBERFORCE: 1759–1833; GURNEY: 1788–1847. That eminent and excellent Friend, Joseph John Gurney, recalls, in his interesting volume of "*Reminiscences,*" an interview he had with his friend, William Wilberforce, in the course of which the latter said, with tears in his eyes, "I have nothing whatever to urge but the poor publican's plea, God be merciful to me a sinner!"—"I well remember (Mr. Gurney adds) his own definition of mercy—'having kindness shown to a *criminal.*' Ah, my dear children, if Wilberforce who has been laboring for these fifty years in the cause of virtue, religion, and humanity, can feel himself to be a poor criminal, with no hope or happiness but through the pardoning mercy of God in Christ Jesus, surely we ought all to be bowed down and broken under similar feelings! Such an example may awfully remind us of the Apostle's question: 'If the righteous scarcely be saved, where shall the ungodly and the sinner appear?'"

Adelaide Newton: 1824–1854. The author of *Walking in the Light*, says: "Soon after my conversion I one day expressed my hopelessness of ever being such a Christian as Adelaide Newton; that such a life was 'not for me.' 'Not for you!' exclaimed a friend present. 'Not for you! You may think yourself a very small vessel, but *are you full?*' The admonition sunk into my very soul, and there and then I asked God for grace that I might never again look upon any privilege designed for all, and which any other Christian had, as though it were 'not for me.' By the grace of God, for the fifteen years that have since passed, I do not remember to have discerned any Gospel-blessing offered to all God's children and possessed by any one, without being upon my knees about it till by faith I obtained it. It became a *holy habit* to expect to receive from God as much as any other of His children. When the more full privileges of the Gospel-sanctification dawned upon my soul nearly ten years after my conversion, I did not say, 'Not for me;' but, in the very first moment of my apprehension of them, since 'all the promises of God in Him are yea and in Him Amen, unto the glory of God by us,' *they are mine.*"

This very characteristic paragraph, which comes

in among the experiences we are quoting like a "cross-current," imports that the author's life became, after a while, closely assimilated to that of Adelaide Newton. Not precisely. Her idea of religion was very far away from his. That it was well-nigh of a seraphic type, every one must have felt who has read her biography. A happy, joyous disciple she was, in the midst of manifold physical weaknesses and sufferings; as much in love with God's word and as earnest in delving both devotionally and critically among its treasures, as any professed Biblical exegete; and travelling onward with an assured faith which never lost sight of her Saviour; she nevertheless deeply felt the corruptions within, and went on confessing and wrestling with them to the close. Rarely is it given to a believer to enjoy such complete and prolonged peace. But no part of it came from the delusive conceit that she was free from sin. She shall speak for herself: "God has been leading me in the valley of humiliation of late; and sometimes my spirit has seemed all but crushed. I keep saying to myself as I go about like the leper of old, 'Unclean, unclean!' and can truthfully say, 'I abhor myself.' I suppose I may read in it all the answer to my own prayers; for I have so entreated to be laid low and kept humble, because I felt I was horribly *self-complacent.*" Again, commenting on the loving kindness of God, or, as she translates the word in Ps. 36 : 10, the "overflowing exuberance of His goodness," she adds : "God goes on teaching me that every fresh ray of light from above does but make manifest some fresh evil within me; but instead of occupying one's moments with repetitions of the deplorable depravity which *seems* as if it only increased upon me every day, it is a higher and better occupation to try and catch even a glimpse of the goodness which fills the heart of Christ—is it not?" Again : " I knew very little of conflict the last time I saw you, and very little of sin. The last year or two have taught me much; and painful as it has been, I see the value of learning it. The struggles of the inner man are so real—so entirely Godward (for man sees them not) that one seems by degrees to learn out the value of life, as it brings one into contact with the living God." Again : "I do so like the ups and downs, and all the sudden transitions in the Psalms. They used to trouble me as if they disturbed the beauty of the passage; but now I seem so to enter into them." Again: "How precious the very struggle is betwixt the new man and the old! It at least proves that the strong man armed is not 'keeping his goods' in peace. And such abasing of self too is the means God has used for preparing me to 'see greater things.' It is just the way He dealt with Daniel and Isaiah, is it not?" Again: "Bitter lessons of sin in myself and in those about me, which deepen almost every day and hour, seem to be my necessary portion, ere I can understand what Jesus is as my High Priest."

CHARLES SIMEON: 1759–1836. This series of "experiences" shall be closed with that of *Simeon of Cambridge*, a "man greatly beloved" of God and man. Hearing that a friend had made some remarks upon his habit of giving expression to his religious feelings in "sighs and groans," as if it indicated that "all was not right in his experience," he drew up the following paper. It is given here at large, as being a most interesting narrative, which cannot fail to edify and encourage Christian readers of every name:

"It is now a little above forty years since I began to seek after God; and within about three months of that time, after much humiliation and prayer, I found peace through that Lamb of God who taketh away the sin of the world. About half a year after that, I had some doubts and fears about my state, in consequence of an erroneous notion which I had imbibed from Mr. Hervey about the nature of saving faith. But when I found from better information that justifying faith was a faith of alliance, and not a faith of assurance, my peace returned; because though I had not a faith of assurance, I had as full a conviction that I relied on the Lord Jesus Christ alone for salvation, as I had of my own existence. From that time to the present hour I have never for a moment lost my hope and confidence in my adorable Saviour; for though, alas! I have had deep and abundant cause for humiliation, I have never ceased to wash in that Fountain that was opened for sin and uncleanness, or to cast myself upon the tender mercy of my reconciled God.

"With this sweet hope of ultimate acceptance with God, I have always enjoyed much cheerfulness before men; but I have at the same time labored incessantly to cultivate the deepest humiliation before God. I have never thought that the circumstance of God's having forgiven me, was any reason why I should forgive myself; on the contrary, I have always judged it better to loathe myself the more, in proportion as I was assured that God was pacified toward me. Nor have I been satisfied with viewing my sins, as men view the stars in a cloudy night, one here and another there, with great intervals between; but have endeavored to get, and to preserve continually before my eyes, such a view of them as we have of the stars in the brightest night: the greater and the smaller all intermingled, and forming as it were one continuous mass; nor yet as committed a long time ago, and in many successive years; but as all forming an aggregate of guilt, and needing the same measure of humiliation daily, as they needed at the very moment they were committed. Nor would I willingly rest with such a view as presents itself to the naked eye. I have desired, and do desire daily, that God would put (so to speak) a telescope to my eye, and enable me to see, not a thousand only, but millions of my sins, which are more numerous than all the stars which God himself beholds, and more than the sands upon the sea-shore. There are but two objects that I have ever desired for these forty years to behold; the one is, my own vileness; and the other is, the glory of God in the face of Jesus Christ; and I have always thought that they should be viewed together, just as Aaron confessed all the sins of all Israel whilst he put them on the head of the scape-goat. The disease did not keep him from applying to the remedy, nor did the remedy keep him from feeling the disease. By this I seek to be, not only *humbled and thankful,* but *humbled in thankfulness,* before my God and Saviour continually.

"The consequence of this unremitted labor is, that I have, and have continually had, such a sense of my sinfulness, as would sink me into utter despair, if I had not an assured view of the sufficiency and willingness of Christ to save me to the uttermost. And at the same time I have such a sense of my acceptance through Christ, as would overset my little bark, if I had not ballast at the bottom sufficient to sink a vessel of no ordinary size. This experience has been now so unintermitted for forty years, that a thought only of some defect, or of something which might have been done better, often draws from me as deep a sigh as if I had committed the most enormous crime; because it is viewed by me, not as a mere single grain of sand, but as a grain of sand added to an already accumulated mountain. So deep are my views of my corruption, that I scarcely ever join in the Confession of our Church without perceiving, almost as with my bodily organs, my soul as a dead and putrefied carcass; and I join in that acknowledgment, 'There is no health in us,' in a way that none but God Himself can conceive. No language that

I could use could at all express the goings forth of my soul with those words, or the privilege I feel in being permitted to address the God of heaven and earth in these words, 'Almighty—and most merciful—Father.'

"Hence, then, my sighs and groans when in secret, and which when least thought of by me, may have been noticed by others. And if the Apostle Paul so felt the burthen of sin as to cry, 'Oh wretched man that I am! who shall deliver me from the body of this death?' (Rom. 7 : 24); if he, who had the first-fruits of the Spirit, groaned within himself, waiting for the adoption, to wit, the redemption of the body (Rom. 8 : 23), yea, 'groaned being burthened' (2 Cor. 5 : 4); who am I, that I should not so feel, or so express my feelings; or that I should even wish to be exempt from them? So far am I from wishing to be exempt from them, that I wish and long to have them in a tenfold greater degree; and as already in my daily approaches to the throne of grace, and in my solitude, and in my rides, it is in sighs and groans that I make known my wants to God more than in words, for 'He knoweth the mind of His Spirit speaking in me;' so I desire yet more and more that the Spirit of God may make intercession, both in me and for me, with groanings which cannot be uttered, since words would fail to give them utterance. Rom. 8 : 26.

"But persons mistake who imagine that groans are expressive only of a sense of guilt: they are often the expressions of desire; as David says, 'Lord, all my desire is before thee; and my groaning is not hid from thee' Ps. 38 : 9. And such, I trust, have been many of the groans which I have uttered in secret, and some of which may possibly have been overheard.

"Nor is it on a personal account only that groans are uttered. A minister who knows what it is to 'travail in birth with his people till Christ be formed in them,' will find many occasions of sorrow, as I have of late years. I have had a people, some of whom have ill understood their duty toward me (Heb. 13 : 17) and have constrained me 'to give up my daily account, not with joy, but with grief;' or, as it is in the original, 'with groans.'

"But supposing those impressions of my feelings to have been on a personal account only, and that only from a sense of my unworthiness, I am far from conceiving it to be on the whole an undesirable experience; for by means of it my joys are tempered with contrition, and my confidence with fear and shame. I consider the religion of the day as materially defective on this point; and the preaching of pious ministers defective also. I do not see, so much as I could wish, an holy, reverential awe of God. The confidence that is generally professed does not sufficiently, in my opinion, savor of a creature-like spirit, or of a sinner-like spirit. If ninety-nine out of an hundred, of even good men, were now informed for the first time, that Isaiah in a vision saw the Seraphim before the throne; and that each of the Seraphs had six wings; and then were asked, 'How do you think they employ their wings?' I think their answer would be, 'How? why they fly with them with all their might; and if they had six hundred wings they would do the same, exerting all their powers in the service of their God:' they would never dream of their employing two to veil their faces, as unworthy to behold their God, and two to veil their feet, as unworthy to serve Him; and devoting only the remaining two to what might be deemed their more appropriate use. But I doubt much whether the Seraphs do not judge quite well as they, and serve their God in quite as acceptable a manner as they would, if their energies were less blended with modesty and conscious unworthiness. But whatever opinions the generality of Christians might form, I confess that this is the religion which I love; I would have conscious unworthiness to pervade every act and habit of my soul; and whether the woof be more or less brilliant, I would have *humility* to be the warp.

"I often in my ministry speak of Job's experience, after God had so revealed Himself to him, as proper for all: why then should I not cultivate it myself, and really, truly, deeply, and as before the heart-searching God, 'abhor myself, and repent in dust and ashes?' Job 42 : 6. Can I enter into the spirit of that word *abhor*, and not groan? Or, is that a word which is to have no counterpart in our actual experience? I do not undervalue joy; but I suspect it, when it is not blended with the deepest humiliation and contrition. God has said that 'a broken and a contrite heart He will not despise;' and is that an attainment that is so low and small that I may leave it behind me, as a state that was proper for me forty years ago, but not now? What is meant by a *broken* heart? Would to God that I knew! for with all my groaning I do not know a thousandth part of what it means; and I would not feel my obligation to my Saviour less than I do for ten thousand worlds. Indeed, I consider that this very feeling will constitute the chief felicity of heaven; and that every blessing we there enjoy will be most of all endeared to us as being the fruit of redeeming love. I behold the glorified saints in *heaven* falling on their faces before the throne, whilst they sing praises to their redeeming God (Rev. 5 : 8–15). What then should I do *on earth?* Yea, I behold even *the angels* who never sinned, adoring God in that same posture (Rev. 7 : 11). What then should *I* do, whose whole soul is but one mass of sin and corruption? Finally, God Himself is light, and I am to be as like Him as I can. But what is light? is it not a combination of different rays,—the red, the orange, the yellow, the green, the blue, the indigo, and the violet? Some would think perhaps that they could make better light, if they had the brilliant rays alone: but so think not I; I would have the due proportion of the sombre with the bright; and all in simultaneous motion: and then I think I should more resemble both the created and the uncreated light. At all events, this is my one ambition, to live with one Mary at my Saviour's feet, listening to his words (whilst others are cumbered about the world), and to die with the other Mary, washing His feet with my tears, and wiping them with the hairs of my head."

The witnesses from whom we have now heard, detail, each one, an experience which must stand or fall with that of the apostle in the seventh and eighth of Romans. There is not the slightest reason to apprehend that it will be stigmatized as " God-dishonoring " by any one who has not been ensnared by the Higher Life delusion. To claim as those writers virtually do (V. chap. I.), that the true doctrine of sanctification has been revealed to them, but was hidden from Christians whose names make up the brightest constellations in the Church's firmament, does not savor of any excessive humility. Indeed, we sadly miss in their books those ample traces, which it would be pleasant to meet, of this pre-eminently Christian grace. Considering how largely they discourse of self, it is surprising how little they have to say of their sins. It would be a refreshing alternation to fall now and then upon a passage in which confessions of ill-desert, self-reproaches, godly sorrow for sin, and aspirations for deliverance from the law of sin and death, might admit us to a goodly fellowship with them. But this may not be. They are travelling on a plane so far above that of ordinary pilgrims, that there can be little intercommunion until they all reach the final goal.

Meanwhile it may be well to note that there

are certain features common to all the experiences cited above, which seem to identify them as of God and not of man: (1) They are pervaded throughout with a vein of *penitence*, which, nature itself teaches, must of right enter into the religion of a sinner. (2) The nearer they approach to God, the deeper becomes their sense of sin, and the more vehement their appeals for the cleansing blood. (3) The ceaseless war they wage through life with their own sins, *does not impair their full assurance of hope*. All the more vigorously do they maintain this conflict, and all the more does the necessity for it humble them, that they are assured of the boundless love and unfailing sympathy of their adorable Redeemer. (4) They have less to say of their attainments than of their shortcomings. When they talk of their sins, it is that they may magnify the unsearchable riches of Christ; and of their peace, it is to exalt Him who is their "Peace," and to protest how immeasurably unworthy they are of His favor. (5) The life they are leading, nourishing, as it does, their gratitude, filial confidence, humility, self-distrust, meekness, hatred of sin, and charity, is eminently a happy life; and one which augments its own happiness, by habitually aiming to promote the happiness of others. (6) It is of the essential nature of this experience, that its favored subjects never account themselves to have "attained." So exalted are their views of the Divine majesty and holiness, and of the spirituality of the law, that their best services are, in their esteem, defiled with their own depravity, and need to be sprinkled with the blood of the cross. Whatever their progress in the Christian graces, the stage they have reached seems to them only as the first round of a ladder which, standing on the earth, has its top hidden in heaven. Assured of God's working in them to will and to do of His good pleasure, they work out their salvation with fear and trembling. Neither trusting in themselves nor distrusting God, they "give all diligence to add to their faith virtue; and to virtue knowledge; and to knowledge temperance; and to temperance patience; and to patience godliness; and to godliness brotherly-kindness; and to brotherly-kindness charity." They well know that they are not to be fully arrayed in this goodly vesture in a day; but they also know that "He who has begun a good work in them, will perform it until the day of Jesus Christ." And so, "laying aside every weight and the sin which doth so easily beset us, they run with patience the race set before them, looking unto Jesus, the Author and Finisher of our faith"—not doubting that in His own good time, they will arrive at the city of the great King, cleansed from *all* sin and made *perfect* in holiness.

What remains, Christian Reader, for you and for me, but "the old, old story," of watching and working, praying and striving, wrestling and fighting, all along the King's highway? But with His gracious eye upon us, His arm around us, and His Spirit within us, we shall, at every stage, learn more and more of the glorious sufficiency, the ineffable love, the unchanging faithfulness, and the tender sympathy, of our Divine Immanuel—our Wisdom, our Righteousness, our *complete* Sanctification, and our final and everlasting REDEMPTION. What would you more?

FINIS.

www.ingramcontent.com/pod-product-compliance
Lightning Source LLC
Chambersburg PA
CBHW031342230426
43670CB00006B/414